by William F. Arendt

The personal World War II story of an
infantry platoon leader told in compelling
and bloody detail--from Normandy to the Rhineland
1944-1945

ISBN 0-9640235-1-2
Library of Congress
Cataloging in Publication Division
98-065169

*To the tens of thousands who never returned,
on behalf of those who did--and especially,
from one who remembers.....*

"(Seeing a man break under pressure) is worse than watching death, for you are seeing something more important than a body die. You are seeing the death of a man's spirit, of his pride, of all that gives meaning and purpose to life."

----Gen. Matthew Ridgway, Page 152
Midnight of the Soul

(from The Taste of Courage, by Flowers and Reeves, Harper & Row, 1960)

Cover Photo from
29 Let's Go

The 29th Infantry Division is finally crossing the swollen Roer River in Germany in 1945-- and not without casualties. Within a few hours after this outstanding action photo was taken, the pontoon bridge was hit by a mortar shell and destroyed.

Table of Contents

Chapters	Page

Prologue

---

*There is a Midnight of the Soul, possibly
more than one. Combat infantrymen have felt its
absolute, paralyzing horror, particularly when they
realize there is no way out.*

---

*F*ew of us are allowed to live, let alone participate in what history may call "important times"-- or those brief years when the course of civilization may be changed. I submit that the first half of the 20th century was one of those times. The litany of events included two world wars, a deep, near-universal depression plus astounding technological, scientific and medical advances.

And if we choose, we can narrow those historically important times to the 1940's decade. It was then that the world experienced its significant battle, our Armageddon, with civilization at risk.

It is appropriate for my World War II-reared generation to set down our experiences of those years. Each account is worthy, down to the smallest detail relating to the smallest unit. That is an important reason for this memoir.

I was totally involved in face-to-face violence, killing and destruction in Europe during that war. The years 1944 and 1945 will never be forgotten by my generation, now concluding our tenure in this world (and another good reason for us to write our tales down, now).

My fighting was done as a member of G, or George, Company, 116th Regiment, 29th (Blue and Gray) Infantry

Division, a Virginia-Maryland-Southeastern Pennsylvania national guard outfit. Mobilized early (February 1941), the Blue and Gray was sent to England in 1942 and then, when the fighting began, was landed first in the firestorm of Omaha Beach on June 6, 1944. The outfit nearly never recovered from that early dose of blood-foamed surf.

Lineage of the 116th Regiment dates to the Civil War when it was part of General Jackson's famous Stonewall Brigade, and then known as the Second Virginia Infantry. Later, during World War I, the Virginians fought at Meuse-Argonne and in the Alsace campaign. The regiment's motto of "Ever Forward" also characterized its performance from Normandy through Germany during World War II.

By the time I joined it in early August, 1944, the Blue and Gray had suffered more than 7,000 casualties, roughly three times the Division's total strength in front-line riflemen. From Omaha Beach through Normandy's St. Lo and Vire, it had struggled virtually without relief or rest. Replacements for the fallen, yes. They always came and went. I was one of that crowd.

By August, there were few Virginians left in the 116th. And in truth, there were up to four 29th Divisions of rifle platoon personnel--one group fighting on line, another in the hospital and roughly two more coming or going. This was not unusual for active infantry divisions in those hedgerow battling days; medical science has done wonders in patching up wounded soldiers and sending them back to duty since World War I. Without that resource, our infantry divisions would cease to exist as fighting units within a few weeks of heavy combat. The replacement system saved our unit identity skins during World War II.

There's a second motivation--and even a third, which I'll cover later in this prologue--for dredging memories and blurred, dimming files for this story: I want to leave something for my family.

First, a caveat. My small piece of World War II in the Stonewall Brigade involved no grand decisions--nor probably, even small ones--affecting the course of that war. I did what I had to do, I hope responsibly. Even the two relatively brief tours I had with the regiment are not cohesive history. My corner of World War II was small, my role as a replacement platoon leader forgettable to everyone but to me and my family.

Platoon leaders (lieutenants or, at times, sergeants) are, however, vital to any army. We may not see past the next hill or the next river, but if we failed to take those objectives, then the entire attack fails. And if we fail to defend well with our small units, then the entire front's defense system shows cracks, likely turning into gaping fissures.

But back to motivations for these memoirs. Early in my life I, like millions of other youngsters, looked, literally, high up to a great-grandfather. My particular hero then was a white-bearded Civil War veteran known as Stephan Fuller. He was at Shiloh, a member of an Illinois artillery battalion, and he was hurt when he was hit by a careening, out-of-control caisson belonging to that unit. He had a limp and a story to tell, and all I ever got was what I saw, a limp. He didn't want to talk about the war, even to an eager seven-year-old listener--and then he died in 1927, with his memories.

I also remember my oldest son, Bill, more recently asking me what was important in my life up to then., then being around my sixtieth year. I responded with the usual "family, children, jobs" and then I said, "as for something that has touched me and probably molded me more than anything, it's been my World War II experience, even though I didn't realize it at the time."

He later claimed that what I actually said was that nothing really important has happened to me since World War II. And strange as that sounds, it may be at least partially true. Not only for me, but for my entire family, and possibly, theirs.

My second son, Steven, was the spark-inceptor of this project. He wanted something to remember, something to hold and show to his kids, coming from both his mother, a Belgian native, and his father. Not too much to ask. So I promised to do this. I was the only person who could. His mother had died in 1988. Besides, I reasoned, my family deserves more than my silence, as they've had to take their Civil War forebear's silence, on events touching their roots.

So much for the primary reasons for his book. As a personal recollection it will not fall heir, hopefully, to a memoir's greatest fault: The alignment of facts and incidences to reflect the shining image of the storyteller. "Not-so-proud-of" moments are recounted here, but I hope not in lurid detail. There's a lot of B and B--Booze and Broads--in this history, simply because that's what most of us thought the most about at that particular stage in our lives. Many of us later became at least somewhat productive citizens, although I still deeply suspect that it was our generation who opened the doors--or certainly allowed them to be opened by our own baby-boom youngsters and their families--to sex, drugs (including alcohol) and violence. After all, these certainly were a big part of our lives in the 1940's. I get guilt pangs often when I watch what's happening to our nation these days. My generation may have started us down the wrong path more than 50 years ago, although all soldiers since the beginning of time were laws unto themselves.

My greatest fear in this book is that I may have missed conveying the excitement of World War II times. There is a tub-thumping magic to a patriotic war difficult to explain in these days of disbelief. When a 1940's youngster donned a military uniform, or took a job in the war effort, he or she was extremely motivated, part of a heroic mass lemming-like movement to one goal--winning.

And in combat, when killing became an early, formative years occupation, then basic "how-to-survive" thoughts became primary icons. While vital for the times, I'm sure those life styles crushed a lot of normal, finer sensibilities, including understanding and sympathy, for a good part of my generation.

Such an emotional swale was hard to climb out of, even years after the end of our war. In my opinion, Vietnam veterans were not the first to experience an attitudinal jet lag in returning to civilian life. And I suspect this alienation feeling by veterans even existed back in post-Civil War days. After all, who in civilian life can ever understand a battlefield? And who in a fight for his life can explain all of the feelings involved?

Writing about events more than 50 years later is not nearly as difficult as it might appear. Some people and events come to mind easily; several others need only a bit of prompting from old letters and notes, unit action histories and official George Company morning reports (required daily logs of unit strength, location and activity) pulled from the voluminous government file box in St. Louis. True, quite a few things are lost forever. I have an empty memory chest of several weeks duration during the early winter of 1944-1945 when I was, like everyone else, hibernating in German basements, waiting to cross the Roer River. Possibly I slept most of that time. I know I didn't much care what happened, and that was a marked change from the gung-ho platoon leader I was before my first wound.

Those years of delayed writing do contribute perspective, too. I now can look at campaigns critically. And who has a better right to critique military decisions than the so-called grizzled and scarred participant?

A great part of this book is, necessarily, hyped memory and reconstruction of conversations and events that may not be entirely accurate but follow my best senses of what was happening at the time. Much of it is opinion-- and not only my own.

A primary reference was the division's own history, *29 Let's Go!*, ably written by Joe Ewing, once a platoon leader in another Blue and Gray regiment, the 175th. Most of the photos and maps used in this book sourced back to the Ewing book and the Infantry Journal Press, its initial publisher. Now in its fifth printing, this hard cover, detailed account of the Blue and Gray's part in World War II is available through the 29th Division Association, Box 74, Blue Ridge Summit, PA. 17214. Appropriately, the cost is $29, plus $3 shipping.

Other sources included the memoirs of Generals Eisenhower and Bradley, Martin Gilbert's *The Second World War*, John Toland's *Battle, the Story of the Bulge*, and a well-detailed *Hitler's Last Gamble* by Jacques Nobecourt.

Additional World War II authors and historians researched included Charles Brown MacDonald, John

Strawson, Martin Blumenson, Kenneth Macksey, David
Eisenhower, Carlo D'Este, Robert Leckie, Desmond Flower
and James Reeves, James Bentley, David Chandler with
General James Lawton Collins, Richard Ernest Dupuy, W.
Dennis and Shelagh Whitaker, Cornelius Ryan, Irwin
Shaw, Field Marshall Viscount Bernard Montgomery and,
in detail, Stephen E. Ambrose, the American historian-
author who wrote so insightfully and emotionally of D-
Day and who now has completed another wartime book
on Northern European campaigns (*Citizen Soldiers*).

Warren Hecker, a retired colonel now living in
Alexandria, Virginia, and a chap who trod the weary
replacement depot trail with me, was an invaluable asset
for this effort--and one of the true treasures I found while
making it. Warren and I recently rekindled a friendship
started in Normandy's hedgerows 53 years earlier.

Background reference works included studies of
the 116th Regiment contained in Henry Kyd Douglas's *I
Rode With Stonewall,* John Overton Cassler's *Four Years in
the Stonewall Brigade* (both Civil War books), *Fighting
Soldier* by Joseph Douglas Lawrence and Edwin Vaughan's
Some Desperate Glory (both World War I books).

My best source--and, in fact, inspiration outside of
my family--was Colonel Charles R. Cawthon, my former
battalion commander whose book *Other Clay* detailed our
Second Battalion struggles from D-Day on. Colonel
Cawthon also retired to Alexandria, Virginia, and often
reflected "on those days of youth and glory that I doubt
we gave much thought to at the time."

A model for the true Southern gentleman he
always was, Colonel Cawthon passed on in mid-1996,
quietly and with the dignity he deserved. As former
Captain Bob Garcia of E Company wrote: "Wouldn't it be
a wonderful world if we could all have the same sense of
decency, compassion and fortitude that that outstanding
man demonstrated to us?"

I don't need to repeat here that there is a special
bond between people who share the risk of death on a
battlefield, whenever and wherever. Although I never met
Charles Cawthon in his later years, we corresponded
regularly. I remember him in battle--lean, intense and
demanding, probably more demanding of himself than

people like me who came and went like the morning sun. But I'll always remember him in recent years encouraging me to do this writing. His comments on the early drafts are treasures of gentleness, understanding and wit.

If there need be another reason for writing this book it is to offer more knowledge of what war is like for the U. S. Infantry rifle platoon member. These people are at any battle's "cutting edge, where it is most shocking, dangerous and decisive. The most extreme experience a human being can go through is being a combat infantryman . . ." as Stephen Ambrose writes in his *D-Day, June 6, 1944: The Climatic Battle of the 2nd World War.*

I have tried to tell it like it was for me and others on the "cutting edge," but I doubt that those who were not there can ever really understand the unforgiving, almost always-cruel elements of nature we constantly faced, the cascading fears and the misery and absolute resignation often with us, sometimes all of them occurring at the same times. Most of us tried not to let emotions bother us or to show that they bothered us--but they were always there. And we often feared that they might become unchained in our straight-arrow, "army-regulations" mindset and send us howling into the night.

Yes, Virginia, there is a Midnight of the Soul, possibly more than one. Combat infantrymen have felt its absolute, paralyzing horror more than once, particularly when they realized there was no way out.

Let it also be said that it is not the length of time spent on the battlefield, but the intensity of that time. My relative few days (and nights) spent leading one advance element of the American assault on Fortress Brest far outperform the weeks I spent waiting and sleeping in Western Germany.

I still carry four deeply-branded impressions or, in my mind, truisms, of infantry combat during World War II: 1) An individual's wartime experiences were generally good or bad depending on his small unit leadership (that means corporals, sergeants and lieutenants--any officers above the rank of lieutenant were rarely, if ever in my experience, seen where the actual fighting was) 2) Actions by a few, sometimes even one man, could and often did change the outcome of any combat situation, 3) Units with a proud history of battlefield success usually performed well at all times (unit pride in the armed services is important, I learned, even though it seems somewhat silly at times) and 4) No matter how bad someone thinks he's had it, somebody else believes he's had it worse (and he's probably right!)

In a memorable quote from *Other Clay*, Colonel Cawthon said: "Make no mistake about it, however, each man's war is separate and personal unto himself and not exactly like that of any other. It is fought first within his own heart and soul and the outcome often is buried with his bones."

I agree heartily. Charles Cawthon's bones are resting easier, and mine will, too, with the telling of our tales of war in the Twentieth Century, our generation's century of memory.

Background

*If you were from Chicago in those days, most
Europeans thought you were a gangster.*

No special talents or background were needed for
an infantry platoon leader during World War II. Mine
were most ordinary, except they did include a love and
respect for nature--given to me by my outdoorsman father.
And yes, there was leadership. I realized early on that I
liked to control everything around me, if I could. I still do.

I was born in Chicago (and delighted to tell my
war-time Belgian friends, who later were to play such an
important role in my life), about my gangster career. This
happened because all Belgians--and Europeans for that
matter--equated Chicago with Al Capone, guns and
prohibition violence. They actually brought people over to
faire une connaissance avec l'homme de Shee-cah-go. The
stories got better as the nights went on and the bottles
were emptied and memories lubricated.

In truth, my family left the big city when I was a
pre-schooler, moving to the small, northwestern Iowa
town of LeMars where my folks set up a millinery and
ladies accessories store. This was homecoming for Dad,
who was born and raised in Plymouth County, Iowa. He
had left in his teens and had done well until a mini-
depression hit the millinery business in the early 1920's.
Both he and my mother arrived in LeMars with not much
more than a will to set up a business. The trust of my

father's colleagues in allowing the young couple credit enabled them to start again--and they were successful until they retired 25 years later.

My first lasting memory of LeMars was of neighborhood kids teasing me for not walking on grass to get a ball they had intentionally thrown into the middle of a large, green yard. In the Chicago apartment complex where we lived, kids were not allowed on the grass, and in LeMars it became good neighborhood sport to watch the little guy from Chicago gingerly tip-toe on the grass and run scared to retrieve a ball. It took my mother to tell me that this sort of rule didn't apply in Tall Corn Iowa--and I was delighted to discover my new freedom, as I well remember.

My father and mother had married late in life (both were in their middle thirties when they had me, their only child). My father was the youngest son of Peter Arendt who immigrated with his family from Luxembourg in the mid-1800's to farm, first in an area near Dubuque, Iowa, then near LeMars in the far northwest corner of the state. Peter broke away from farming, however, and served as the elected sheriff of Plymouth County for a dozen years in the early 1900's. He had long retired when I arrived on the scene, but I remember him as big, gruff and burly with a huge mustache and an overpowering tobacco smell. Also, he had a gold watch and chain parked on a huge belly which I recall pulling at frequently.

My father began his career as a Western Union telegraph operator, working Morse Code at various railroad towns over Iowa and Minnesota. He finally settled in Illinois where he worked the Associated Press market wire for the Chicago Board of Trade.

When his hearing loss began in his mid-twenties (although he had always been deaf in one ear from an untreated childhood disease) he decided to look for other work, mainly because he couldn't keep pace with the fast and exacting AP wire. He took a job as a traveling salesman for millinery companies, most of them importers of flowers, beads, feathers and other ladies' hat and dress accessories. One of his stops was in Topeka, Kansas, where he found my mother making and selling hats in a large department store's millinery department.

The courtship, I was told, was long and difficult, not only because of distance but also because Edith, my mother, was a disciple of Victorian virtue. She was chaperoned by her rooming house landlady, ironically named Mrs. Robinson.

Mrs. Robinson was Edith's surrogate mother, a family friend who inserted herself into Edith's life almost at birth, when Edith's mother died. At that time, my mother's father took off for the Colorado gold fields and left his little girl with his parents, Stephan and Margaret Fuller, and later, the ever-present Mrs. Robinson. I remember meeting Charles, Edith's father, as a seven or eight year-old. I thought he was a great story-teller. To my mother he was a wastrel and vagabond drunk.

One other important point here. I was the only child on either side of the family--my mother was an only child and my father's brother and sisters remained single-- or, in the case of one uncle and one aunt, married but with no children.

I learned early the values of shopping around, where a "no" may turn into a "yes" if asked of the right adult at the right time.

Despite this, I don't think I was spoiled. My mother was a strict disciplinarian. There were no surplus toys and certainly little or no coddling. I was on my own in Iowa, mostly with a housekeeper guardian while my parents worked long hours in the millinery store.

Like many other youngsters in those barnstorming years, I was fascinated by airplanes. I remember helping to carve dozens of models, of trading them for others and even trying to fly gliders from tree to tree with secret messages. My best pre-10-year-old Christmas, I recall, was when I received a carved, solid wooden model of a World War I bomber, a biplane with rear-mounted engines behind a bow turret machine gun. It was big, blue and beautiful.

First memories of the newspaper business were linked with ice and snow and early Sunday morning darkness in Northwest Iowa a half-dozen years later. The *Des Moines Sunday Register* had to be delivered early although why, at that hour on a motionless and paralyzing cold winter morning, I'll never understand. My route was in hilly, southeast LeMars. I remember taking as few as five to 10 papers in my wire handlebar bicycle basket and mushing up a snowy, slippery incline. Sometimes it took me three or four tries, but I generally finally made it, if necessary crawling over snowdrifts in yards to avoid the icy streets and sidewalks.

Then I would go back and get another pile from my 55-paper allotment and try another hill. I never quit, because that would be a disgrace for me, my family and the family friend who hired me.

I still remember the joy of early Sunday mornings in the spring, summer and fall, however. Alone in a church-like silence, the world slept. There was a feeling of power. Despite all this pristine beauty and appeal, I kept the paper delivery job for only a year or two. I guess winter struggles outweighed the good times. Maybe I decided I was too busy in school. Or more likely, my folks tired of getting up on Sunday mornings.

It was only in my later, high school years, that I developed an interest in the writing side of newspapering. After I took a part-time printer's devil job in the back shop of a local semi-weekly, I began to write the scores, then stories on the high school football and basketball games, despite the fact that I was a reserve on both teams, a tuba player in the band and, at times, an actor, choir boy and cheerleader. Always a participant, I never really developed significant skills at anything in those days.

After high school I attended the local college, then called Western Union (always worth a chuckle in later years when people asked about my background) and later named Westmar University. All true colleges these days seem to like the rolling sound of the word university-- probably because it rolls in more money (this didn't work for Westmar, however; the school was forced to close in 1998 for lack of same). During those years I developed my first job as a sports reporter and columnist for the *LeMars Semi-Weekly Sentinel*. At the same time and apparently in harmony with my then-current philosophy of keeping busy all the time, I was soliciting advertisements for a competing semi-weekly, the *LeMars Globe-Post*. Each management certainly knew about this double employment--they both paid me 25 cents an hour! I also recall some in-lieu-of-salary payments from the *Sentinel* for my sports writing prose amounting to 5 cents per column inch. No wonder I became wordy.

About this time a great aunt, Mary Arendt from Des Moines, took an interest in me as a potential bright spot in what she obviously and mistakenly considered an otherwise dull family group.

Aunt Mary had all the credentials to make judgments--age and experience, street-wise common sense--and money. And she wasn't shy.

She got most of her money from her long-time companion, Judge Charles C. Bradley, with whom she cohabited after her husband, John, died in the 1920's. There were some gossips in LeMars who had her sleeping with the judge before Uncle John, a traveling man, died. The judge was a bachelor roomer with Aunt Mary and Uncle John for many years.

Charles Bradley, a gentle man who looked like a judge, was known as the "nearly hanged" district judge of the farm revolution in Iowa in the early 1930's.

Irate farmers literally pulled him off his courthouse bench on April 27, 1933 and took him in an open truck to a field a mile or so east of town. He was blindfolded and a rope put around his neck. Asked that he promise never to foreclose another mortgage, the judge refused and began praying aloud that "justice be done." Later the angry farmers took off his clothes, smeared oil over his body with the intention of a tar and feather application and then released him. Some of the locals said the farm leaders were impressed by his refusals to bend.

Judge Bradley became a hero in the LeMars community. But he was wrecked, physically and emotionally. He resigned from the bench and took the trustee job to merge the Royal Union Life Insurance Company of Des Moines into the Lincoln Life Company. As the merged companies began investing in the slowly-awakening stock market in the later 1930's so did Judge

Bradley--and so did Aunt Mary, still at his side. They did well.

When the judge died, he left everything, or most everything, to Aunt Mary. She moved back to LeMars and purchased a large home on a hill near the college. Well into her eighties by now, Aunt Mary continued to smoke her cigarettes and drink her shots of whiskey, mostly neat.

Eventually, my family moved in with her. I became a favorite of hers. The judge's large library, which she moved from Des Moines, became one of my biggest hangouts. I discovered the judge liked pornography, Huxley and all. I was exploring sex and fortunately, other things in his books, a good deal of my spare time.

About this time there were serious family discussions of what Bill Junior, me, was going to do with his life. I wanted journalism, and Aunt Mary offered to help pay my way through the top-grade Medill J-School at Northwestern University.

It was a turning point in my young life, and like so many others of tender years, I never realized at that time what an education from a prestige school would eventually mean. I did appreciate what my aunt did for me; as the years passed, we became buddies and confidants. When she died in the late 1940's (she never gave her age, but the family guessed she was 97 or 98) I truly grieved--and I hadn't done that since my platoon radio man died in my arms in France.

My last two years of college at Northwestern were mostly a struggle to keep going. I had jobs at the now-defunct *Evanston News-Index,* the Chicago City News Bureau, the school library, a Feltman-Curry shoe store in Evanston, the Scott Hall Cafeteria, plus a hashing job in the Alpha Phi sorority house before I got a writing assignment with Stewart Howe Alumni Services. I happily edited sorority and fraternity news letters thereafter.

I didn't stay for Northwestern's 1942 graduation ceremonies. I had squeaked through the last semester after Pearl Harbor and got my degree with little thought on education and more on wartime service.

Two Phi Gamma Delta fraternity brothers and I began hitch-hiking to California in early May. We rode freight trains, slept in a 25-cents-a-night flophouse in Green River, Wyoming, and did ice-loading for the Pacific Fruit Express in Sparks, Nevada. Our mission was simple: We wanted to see a bit of the world before--not after--we entered the service.

We ended our journey in Berkeley, at the University of California. I began working the swing shift at Kaiser's Richmond ship yards and monitored some classes in history at UC-Berkeley. Mostly I had fun in San Francisco.

All of this was great--I even fell in love a couple of times--but I recognized there was an Iowa draft board with my number. By fall, I hadn't been called. Nor did it seem likely soon, they said in their best "we-have-you-hooked-why-hurry?" manner. So I decided to volunteer and took the next train back to Iowa. This time I didn't ride the rods.

I had no dreams of service in anything but the Army. Even into basic training I anticipated duty in the infantry--and that was just about right. I knew how to shoot, liked the outdoor life and figured, rightly, that this was where the war was going to be fought and won.

The limited edition Arendt family, circa 1926. Father William Grover was a millinery salesman out of Chicago; when things went bad in the big city he took his wife and son to LeMars, Iowa, his family's home, and set up shop. The Billy Arendt Hat Shop endured for 30-plus years next to the Royal Theater in downtown LeMars and became a unique oasis for women from miles around this Northwest Iowa farming community. Both of my parents were married relatively late in life and had me when they were in their mid-thirties. Because of his hearing difficulties and a consequent ability to concentrate, my father became an excellent bridge and chess player. My mother was always stylish and somewhat aloof. Her moral standards remained high--too high for me at times. In those early years, I was always a little embarrassed to see my father in the ladies hat and accessory store (why couldn't he have been a cattle feeder, or even a druggist?) but I later realized what an excellent combination he and my mother made--she the creative hat maker, he the charmer sales person and wise money man and buyer. Their venture was successful, but they only had serious retirement-type funds after Aunt Mary died in 1949.

The Famous Aunt Mary with her favorite (and only) grand nephew (upper left). Aunt Mary never told her age. The family all thought she was near 100 when she died shortly after WWII, slugging whisky and smoking cigarettes to the end. The snow shoveling and choir pictures (me in the middle) are probably not representative, although by today's standards I was a paragon of hard work and familial devotion. I certainly was into everything, but excelled at little or nothing.

World War II—Table of Organization

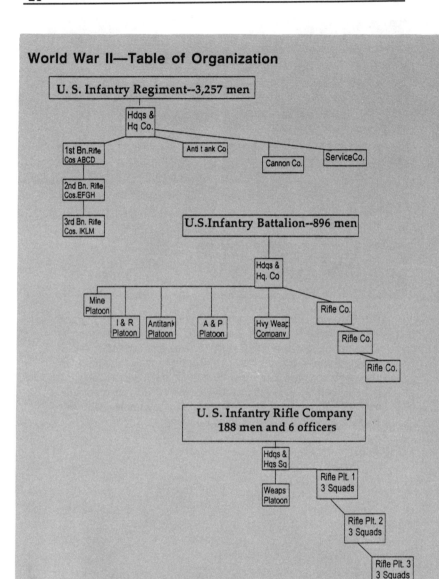

U. S. Infantry Regiment--3,257 men

Hdqs & Hq Co.

- 1st Bn. Rifle Cos. ABCD
- 2nd Bn. Rifle Cos. EFGH
- 3rd Bn. Rifle Cos. IKLM
- Anti tank Co
- Cannon Co.
- Service Co.

U.S. Infantry Battalion--896 men

Hdqs & Hq. Co

- Mine Platoon
- I & R Platoon
- Antitank Platoon
- A & P Platoon
- Hvy Weap Company
- Rifle Co.
- Rifle Co.
- Rifle Co.

**U. S. Infantry Rifle Company
188 men and 6 officers**

Hdqs & Hqs Sq

- Weaps Platoon
- Rifle Plt. 1 3 Squads
- Rifle Plt. 2 3 Squads
- Rifle Plt. 3 3 Squads

History and Tactics

The U. S. infantry division was triangularized, streamlined and fortified in firepower in the early 1940's, marking the end of the "squared" division--two brigades of at least two regiments each--and primarily employed in the trench warfare of World War I. The new units were created for tactical maneuverability capabilities.

The basic platoon fighting unit had three squads of 8 to 12 men each; the company had three rifle platoons and a weapons platoon; the battalion three rifle companies, a heavy weapons company and headquarters company; the regiment three battalions and, of course, the division (total authorized strength: 14,352 men including elements of all the combat arms: artillery, engineers, armor and, of course, infantry supported by heavy weapons and special task units) had three regiments, each with more than 3,000 men.

Common battlefield tactics during World War II were to have two units forward (initially in direct frontal contact, no more than 20 to 25 men per rifle platoon--two squads--most often less) and one unit in reserve for manuevering, although any combination of one up or two up, or even three up, could be used effectively according to the battlefield situation.

Customized units with added support firepower, called combat teams, often were created by regiments or divisions for specialized tasks. In practice, most of U. S. infantry units during World War II fought at two-thirds to half strength, sometimes even less. British divisions, especially late in the war, and all German divisions if they had been in battle, were fortunate if they had 30 per cent of their authorized strength.

--Chart information supplied by U. S. Army's Infantry Journal Press

One of my brief but memorable friendships from World War II includes this man, Warren Hecker, now of Alexandria, Virginia. Then he was a recent West Point graduate, thrown into battle, like me, as a replacement to exhausted men. Hecker and I bunked together in the 86th Replacement Battalion (a manpower holding unit) for a week as we waited assignment. We never saw each other again and only renewed acquaintantships as I began writing this book--a bonus event I had never counted on.

Col. Hecker (ret.) then and now (lower right). He has one of the few photos (upper right) of Koslar, Germany, taken in November, 1944, just after its fall to the 29th. . Charlie Company,115th Rgt. officers (right) as of Feb., 1945, were (l to r) Lieuts. Stoen, Hecker, Blalock and Button. Hecker later was a Second Division battalion commander in Korea and before retiring, headed the Army's Intelligence School for the Pacific Theater. He holds two Purple Hearts and combat infantry badges, plus several uncounted wounds and eight valor awards, all from his World War II and Korean service.

*--Photos courtesy
Warren Hecker*

1

Omaha Beach--Still Pushing

*On D-Day the Germans could have killed everything
living on Omaha Beach; maybe they simply ran
out of ammunition or were just lousy shots--or
even tired of their shooting gallery massacre*

*E*ight weeks after D-Day Omaha Beach was still a scrambled junkyard, but a working one. Here, the landscape-monster stretching in front of me as far as I could see, was World War II's largest killing field--a narrow, crescent strip of mud and sand and stones framed by dusty brown cliffs extending to infinity on either side.

The front ramp of my LCT (Landing Craft Tank) had just clanked down on a steel and concrete pier extending into the Channel. It was my first step into France and much different than what had happened here on June 6, 1944.

I was part of the constant stream of replacements for the dead, wounded and missing of the Allied ground forces in Normandy. There must have been more than 40 of us jammed into that oversized bathtub of a boat.

We had just crossed the English Channel on a pre-war tourist trade packet, off-loaded to our LCT's and headed for the beach. We were either fresh from England or the United States, ready to add our bodies and souls to the war effort in Europe. And our first look at that conflict, to me anyway, was impressive.

To our right front, as the ramp fell, was the *Les Moulins* draw, one of the few primary routes to the top of the cliffs. D-8 Cats with ravaging blades and gutteral power were still working on a curving path-roadway but they didn't slow the stream of traffic upward. Pale gray barrage balloons dotted a darker gray, mid-morning sky. To our right and rear were several freighters lashed to a pier forming a square and extending hundreds of yards into the sea. Further out a line of half-sunken ships and war debris formed a breakwater.

As we crossed the beach to the road, we could see part of the D-Day leftovers. Pieces and parts of every war tool imaginable were reaching out of the sand or propped against more useless discards. I saw at least three or four twisted 105-howitzers and blackened half-tracks, even several 2 1/2-ton trucks, sand-buried at crazy angles. Some were well out from the tide's high water edge, still well-marked by more invasion debris. Hedgehogs and other beach obstacles dotted the scenery in either direction.

But despite the signs of a military disaster, which D-Day almost was, Omaha Beach now was a bustling, move-it type of place. And nobody, possibly except new arrivals like us, was stopping to gape.

We formed two columns and walked up either side of the *les Moulins* "road"--tough going over rough terrain up a steep hill. I was just glad no one was shooting at us. We paused near the top and I had a chance to look down at the beach from the German D-Day viewpoint. Right then I decided that the only way our guys made it that day was because of some German oversight or carelessness in not shooting every moving thing lying helpless below. Or maybe the Krauts ran out of ammunition or were just bad marksmen. I tried to imagine what it must have been like that early morning just a little over a month ago when a thunderstorm of steel welcomed Americans to France.

"Those guys were spread-eagled on the sand and couldn't even see what was killing them," I remarked to a soldier next to me.

And I remembered reading that each man in the assault regiments, the 116th of the 29th Division and the

16th of the First Division, was carrying nearly 90 pounds of equipment. They were then dumped in chest-deep water, most of them seasick from the long rough water ride from England. Add to that pitching of the landing craft, the cold and the misery.

As one historian later commented, "even the best-conditioned athletes in the world could not go careening around a beach under those heavy-load and sick circumstances."

Our group was on its way to the 86th Replacement Battalion, feeder organization of V Corps, First Army, and consisting of the two D-Day divisions, the First and 29th. Both divisions were still fighting, thanks to the constant stream of replacements from the 86th. They were, on this late July date, just east of St. Lo, about 30 miles from Omaha Beach. We didn't know it at the time, but the great Patton breakthrough was just beginning; the Germans were starting to run.

As we rested at the top of the Omaha cliffs, waiting for our trucks, I noticed for the first time the sickening, sharp and semi-sweet stench of battlefield death--the first of too many times for me. It was from the carcasses of cows. Bloated and stiff-legged, their remains evidently were pushed over the cliffs to rest midst the rest of the war's debris on the hillside below. I've never forgotten that smell.

From on top, the sunken ship breakwater looked irregular with ships and wrecks of ships pointed every which direction.

"I guess they had a helluva storm here last week. Knocked the shit out of everything," a lieutenant with our group announced. "We weren't supposed to come in here, except they had no other place to land us. At least that's what I heard one of our Navy guys say."

"Let's go back and start all over then," another voice responded.

"Maybe this is all a mistake and these trucks are going to take us back to England," another lieutenant cracked. I think it was me, always a bit inclined to mask feelings with weak humor attempts.

A string of trucks, looking like they were competing in a dusty demolition derby, rolled up about that time. Sure enough, they were from the 86th. We loaded in a hurry. No one wanted to stick around such an attractive target as that busy beach.

The German Luftwaffe was still active, at certain times in certain places, and Omaha Beach was a prime target. One thing I noticed before we left was the spotting of many of our anti-aircraft guns in former German concrete emplacements. Those guns became active later, particularly at night. Much of their spent ammunition fragments fell on our positions during the next week, even though we were several miles from the beach defensive area.

German prisoners were digging new gun positions as we watched. G. I.'s guarding them had their rifles at port, in front of them, ready for action. They must have been on constant alert, and we saw similar scenes repeated as we moved inland.

"Let's get moving," someone shouted as I swung into the cab of a hastily loaded, already-beginning-to- roll Army truck. The driver didn't need any encouragement. He made this trip at least twice daily, he said, and he never really wanted to stop his truck. Just yesterday, he reported, there had been a Jerry air raid.

"One lonely little Kraut plane got two of your guys and he made only one pass. Every night they're dropping mines around here," he added. I later learned the "mines" he was talking about were anti-personnel fragmentation bombs, a great many of which never exploded.

Our convoy to the replacement depot (we called it a "repple depple") was led by a jeep, followed by at least a dozen troop-packed trucks rolling behind, all at 50-yard intervals and all moving fast on a shell-pocked road. We were headed south and east on what was the Isigny-St Lo national route. But there was no way we could stay on this important artery, We began detouring around the Norman countryside on side roads, sometimes resembling ancient cart paths. I had no idea which direction or heading we were taking. Follow the guy ahead of you and don't ask questions--that was the Army method then, as it probably is even now. And why not? "Follow me" was and remains the Infantry School motto, something we all learned early in our sertvice careers.

I remember well my introductions to this life. Coming back in the fall of 1942 from the California shipyards to Iowa to be drafted, I knew my number was so far down the list that I likely wouldn't be taken for another six or eight months. I also knew Iowa winters and I was positive I didn't want to spend any more time contemplating or attacking snowbanks. So I volunteered for army service that fall, was processed through Fort Des Moines and sent to Camp Joseph T. Robinson in rocky central Arkansas for basic training. Six weeks later I was selected for non-commissioned officers' school. Another few weeks and up came my appointment to Officers Candidate School at Fort Benning, Georgia.

I always liked the Army. Maybe it was because my mother encouraged me with World War I pictures and stories (she went with an aviator, a West Point graduate, before she married my father) or, more likely, it was because I was always a fascinated student of armed conflict dating back to grade school, when I avidly studied the Roman Wars, the Civil War and World War I picture books.

Following graduation from Fort Benning (five months after I joined the services) I was assigned to the Fifth Infantry Regiment, just returning to the states after nearly 20 years duty in Panama. I reported to the Fifth at Camp Carson, Colorado. We were a part of the 71st Light Infantry Division, specialized mountain and jungle fighters. We had no motorized transport, only mules. And we carried all of our supplies on our backs on pack boards. We had reduced manpower and firepower compared to a regular Army division. Each unit was cast to live on its own, isolated, for days at a time.

We trained for more than a year around Colorado Springs. Then we went to Hunter Liggett Military Reservation in California, a hilly, mesquite-covered desolation wilderness in the coast range near Camp Roberts, west of a crossroads called King City, next to William Randolph Hearst's San Simeon and the Pacific Ocean. Nearly every step on that vine-tangled, precipitous ground required the swing of a machete.

Our light division concept was basically abandoned after field exercises at Hunter Liggett proved it took more than 20 days to bring all three of our regiments on line from a start less than 10 miles away. We just didn't have the heavy equipment to deal with difficult terrain and the need to position our larger-caliber firepower.

From our dissolved light infantry division came the cadre for the 10th Mountain Division (which later fought well in Italy and is considered one of our better active divisions today), and much of the core group to reform the 71st as a regular, triangularized division (it fought in Europe later), plus a group of volunteers for General Merrill's ill-fated Marauders in Burma. Only a few of this group ever made it back from forced marches, malaria and months of starvation in that Asian jungle.

I almost volunteered for the Merrill group, but changed my mind at the last moment because I had found a new girl friend in Colorado Springs and really didn't want to leave that delightful city. So much for that hopeful romantic liaison. Within a month I had special orders to return to Fort Benning and prepare for overseas shipment as a replacement officer. My orders came just after D-Day.

I left Boston a few days later on the superfast liner, the West Point, formerly known as the SS United States. She was this country's civilian speed challenger to the Queen Elizabeth on pre-war Atlantic runs. Double-loaded, the West Point could carry more than five thousand troops, with half of them in bunks and the other half on deck until the bunks emptied. On return trips the West Point carried German prisoners who cleaned the ship.

We made it to Liverpool within six days, unescorted. The ship's officers convinced us the West Point could outrun any torpedo, and I was just happy we didn't have to prove it. The crossing was great. We knew we were in a hurry.

Once we got to England, however, it was wait, and then wait some more. For two weeks we sat around in a "repple depple" while our invasion forces were fighting from hedgerow to hedgerow to take St. Lo, initially scheduled to fall a few days after the Normandy landing. It was July 18, six weeks after D-Day, when St. Lo finally was captured. And by that time we were on our way to our embarkation port, Plymouth, and finally, to the fighting.

The stay in England was memorable, however. I got to know and appreciate the locals in and around Birmingham. My admiration for the English good humor and their tight little green island, then under siege, mounted. I rapidly became an Anglophile and remain one to this day.

Our first and only stop in Plymouth was at dockside, where we boarded what evidently once was a coastal luxury liner for tourists--planked decks, brass portholes and fittings, wooden railings just right for leaning. All we need was deck chairs! We were to make the Channel crossing at night. Most of us just put our bedrolls on deck and bunked out.

At dawn we were told to climb down rope ladders to get into our landing craft. There were a few jokes about us opening another front because of our invasion-type debarking moves, but it all went well, if somewhat slowly, and the rising sunglow in a bleak sky saw us on our way to Normandy in our LCT--a seaworthiness joke with a ride something akin to that of a ping pong ball in rough bathtub waters. I, for one, didn't much care where we were landing in France. Only after the LCT was underway did I ask the coxswain where we were headed. His answer was one word, "Omaha." I really woke up then.

My wandering mind struggled back to reality when the 86th Replacement Depot truck hit a couple of holes, and I was relieved when the lead jeep suddenly turned off a graveled highway, slowed and took another rutted side road. We were raising dust and I figured that we may attract some incoming artillery until I realized that everyone was on the move this morning and the Germans had little time to shell just another dust-raising motor column. Much too far away, anyway.

At intervals, the trucks would stop as the jeep stopped. We watched our guides consulting maps and gesturing. I hoped we weren't lost--that's one of the worst things that can happen on a battlefield, even this far behind the so-called front lines.

Actually it would not be difficult to get lost in the hedgerow or, as the French called it, le bocage country. Everything looked the same. A small village or a cluster of ruined farm buildings, still occupied by the Normans, could be found at nearly every road intersection. But because the Normans didn't believe in grid systems and their roads followed irregular field patterns, it was difficult to know exactly which direction was which. Anyway, this wasn't my problem--yet.

It did appear that our guide was trying to find his way. We later found out that our trip took abnormally long because he was using the circular approach instead of the Point A to Point B styles we all were taught.

At virtually every stop, if we were near some shattered buildings, these hardy French folk would come out to trade their apple cider, maybe eggs or bread, for our cigarettes. They also had a more potent drinking alcohol called *Calvados*. And it actually worked in cigarette lighters. I tried it.

I found out later that *Calvados* is made by leaving apple cider in its cask for up to two years. Then it is distilled twice and placed in oaken casks laced with apple cores, certainly gaining strength with each passing hour, month and year. The Normans historically drank *Calvados* with their meals to help their digestive process, they said. Some of us thought *Calvados* actually made holes in their stomachs so they could eat more.

I tried a sip or two later on. It didn't quite taste like gasoline, but there was a resemblance. I agreed it would make holes in any normal person's stomach.

The Normans weren't that happy to see us, and I could hardly blame them. We blew up their homes and farms and crops and generally laid waste to a beautiful orchard, dairy and small crop country.

At the same time the Normans were pleased to see the feared Germans leave. Four years of occupation were anything but pleasant and the farmers wanted to twist Kraut tails when *les sals boches* retreated as much, if not more, than we did. Mostly, the staunch and unemotional Normans wanted to be left alone.

When our truck stopped near a Norman farm house and the occupants came spilling out, I tried to talk with them using my textbook French. I had taken two years of the language in college--why I'll never know because it was my toughest subject by far. But I thought I knew it and could use it advantageously then. I really couldn't understand more than a couple of words from any conversation I ever had with the Normans. I presume they couldn't understand me either because nothing ever happened but smiles and handshakes and the continuation of sign language bartering. At that time I put this failure to communicate down to a difference in local dialects, but later I wasn't so sure. A good part of our problem then, I'm now convinced, was because the Normans didn't really want to talk to me with my strange accent and my bludgeoning of their language; it was many months later and under totally different circumstances that I did manage the language somewhat, but that was only after reading newspapers, listening a lot and speaking French as much as possible, plus ignoring my many errors. I've been a believer since those days that classroom studies of foreign languages are mostly a waste of time.

We made it to the replacement battalion after an hour or so of back roading in which we never saw another Allied vehicle. We did see plenty of planes, all of them ours. The Luftwaffe, in defeat, had disappeared for all but sneak raids. German ground troops, except for delaying actions, were trying to get back across the Seine River to establish another defense line. The fighting, or what remained, was miles from us. We thought the war may be over, and just as we were about to swing into action. There were lots of "let-me-at-em" heroes in our replacement group then, and talk was big.

Since those days I've developed several theories about the German Army and, in fact, about the German people. First, they don't give up. Second, they are resourceful, experienced fighters, at their best in a defensive situation not requiring much maneuvering and thirdly, they know how to retreat and still keep order in the ranks--always considered one of the most difficult of military tasks. I should add one more: Always, but always, expect a counterattack after one of their positions has been taken.

Back at the 86th Replacement Battalion we claimed our assigned foxholes and began again--to wait. The battalion had a training program, such as it was, in which we listened to combat tips from some battle-weary sergeants who may not have been present or, if present, sober when class time began. We had night assemblies of weapons, map understanding and reading sessions and early-morning calisthenics, some lectures and then, surprise, movies.

These movies had to be shown in daylight hours, however, because the Germans always put up a light plane over our positions at night.

Bedcheck Charlie was his nickname and creating nervousness was his game. He came over us, with his little putt-putt engine, every night just before midnight, when everything was black outside. Our double summer time kept the sun up until after 9 and twilight was long indeed in this relatively far north latitude.

Sometimes Charlie would drop anti-personnel bombs, basically grenade-sized. Sometimes he would drop leaflets. He would always make our troops a little edgy. We had strict orders not to fire at him so as not to give away our positions; as if he didn't know where we were. He found us every night and stayed with us for what seemed like an hour or two. Actually it was probably 15 minutes.

Cigarette smoking, reading or playing cards-- except under a blanket--were also forbidden when Bedcheck was about. I often wondered how many lights he saw from upstairs and if he knew, for sure, what kind of a unit we were. I suspect he probably saw enough reserve manpower and equipment below him to bring the shakes to the Kraut generals he reported to.

When I first arrived at the "repple depple" I froze whenever I heard Charlie's lawn-mower type motor[1], as if he could see me moving as an individual. Later, all of us got used to Charlie and continued whatever we were doing. A lot of amateur tacticians wanted to get a searchlight and an ak-ak (anti-aircraft) gun and shoot him down, but after a bit they got used to him, too.

My first two weeks of August were spent in the "repple depple" camp. And my only explanation for the

---

[1] Some psycho war people claimed all German engines were unsynchronized on purpose

delay, belatedly reasoned, was that the front was so disorganized at the time that our V Corps replacement supply line was temporarily halted. Many units were being handed over to Patton's Third Army to fuel the all-wheels-forward advance. Replacements would have a hard time catching up with him.

For much of this time, the only fighting units left in V Corps were the 1st and 29th Divisions. They were shortly to receive their first prolonged rest and rejuvenation since D-Day, and the 86th Repple Depple would be the primary blood donor.

I remember my foxhole partner, a West Point lieutenant, had hoped to be assigned to the First Division. It had a glorious history of professionalism in every important U. S. battle since the Revolutionary War--an ideal assignment for a young West Pointer. My new companion was about the same age as I. He turned into a friend and learning source as we went down the replacement trail together.

By this time in my army career I had developed enormous respect for West Point graduates. I had run into a few of them in old Fifth Infantry mountain regiment (also their type of Old Army unit with the requisite number of battle flags) and found quickly that they knew a lot more about this new combat command job of mine than I did.

It was more than just technical knowledge, although small unit battlefield tactics were basic for them. More, West Pointers seemed to develop a magical hold on their men. We all knew that self-assuredness, professionalism and a show of confidence by a leader transmits to the men under him, generally producing ease, smoothness, discipline and ultimately, performance. We've also learned that there were few, if any, ways to teach this to aspiring leaders. Most West Pointers I have known came by these leadership qualities naturally.

My West Point guy (I only remembered his complete name after he wrote me years later: Colonel Warren Hecker, USA Retired) was patient, understanding and had dozens of good suggestions for a 90-day wonder lieutenant who at that time took his army career very seriously.

He was probably one of the individuals closest to me during my combat duty although I never saw him again after that week or 10 days we spent together. Purposefully, I hadn't made many friends since I left the states, mostly because short stays anywhere don't foster friendships. I was not the only one who kept mostly to himself. We were not likely to ever see momentary companions in the replacement pipeline again, so we treated each other as passing ships. I really don't know why Hecker and I hit it off so well. Perhaps we both needed someone to talk to, a friendly face in a threatening world.

I knew that if my West Pointer friend actually requested duty in the First Division, he'd probably get it. The regulars are good at taking care of their own in assignments, as they should be. Theirs is a chosen career. Proper assignments mean a lot.

I asked him to include my name when he requested his First Division posting. He said he would, but I don't think he ever made a request (Warren liked to "go with the flow," he said later). At any rate, I felt good until the list came out the next day. We both were assigned to the 29th-- Warren to the 115th, me to the 116th Regiment. So much for "West Point Pull."

Warren left later that day. I wasn't due out until the next morning. So I got some information on the 29th and I read it all. Then I asked about the 116th. I found my new outfit had an excellent performance record despite the Omaha Beach mauling. And I was ready for the Blue and Gray the next morning. I'm sure they were ready for me-- one more replacement platoon leader in a long, long parade of people who were among the first to fall.

And while I knew all this in the back of my mind, I was eager to get to the task. Call it unknowing bravado, stupidity--anything. Warren called it a "hungering anticipation for one more of life's adventures," something I'm sure he never read in a West Point manual.

I only know that this eagerness, present in thousands of Americans waiting for action at that time, is what won the war.

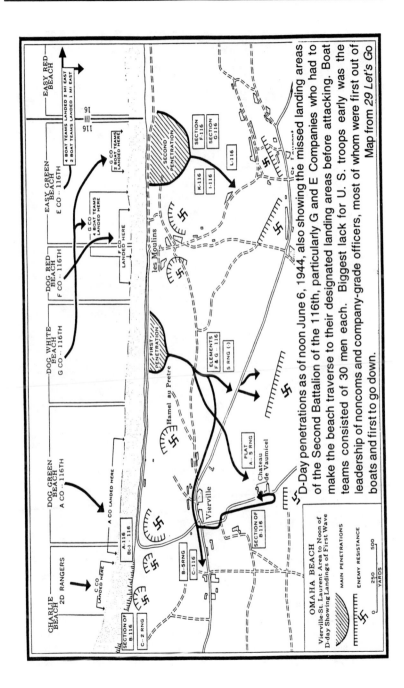

D-Day penetrations as of noon June 6, 1944, also showing the missed landing areas of the Second Battalion of the 116th, particularly G and E Companies who had to make the beach traverse to their designated landing areas before attacking. Boat teams consisted of 30 men each. Biggest lack for U. S. troops early was the leadership of noncoms and company-grade officers, most of whom were first out of boats and first to go down.

Map from 29 Let's Go

Omaha Beach in the late afternoon of D-Day. The St. Laurent crossroads (pointing arrow) is under attack. German positions are shown at lower left. The 116th was tied up here through midnight until the Division reserve, the 115th, could get ashore and join the battle via the E-1 beach access route.   --Photo from *29, Let's Go*

Deutſche Allgemeine Zeitung

Berlin, Mittwoch, 7. Juni 1944　　83. Jahrgang 7.6.W　Nr. 155　20 Pfennig

Die Invasion hat begonnen
Abwehr und Kampf in vollem Gange

Ueberraschung mißlungen

Luftlandeverbände in der Seine-Bucht abgesetzt — Landungsboote an anderen Abschnitten der Küste — ˙Geschütze des Atlantik-Walls im Kampf mit feindlichen Kriegsschiffen

Entscheidungskampf

The Berlin press reports the landings: "The Invasion Has Begun . . . Battle and Defense in Full Swing." Headlines over the map read, "Surprise Fails . . . Paratroopers Dropped in the Seine Estuary—Landing Craft Hits Other Sections of Coast—Guns of the Atlantic Wall in Battle with Enemy Warships."

The Berlin press reports the landings (erroneously)-- "The Invasion Has Begun. . . . Battle and Defense in Full Swing. Surprise Fails. Paratroopers Dropped in the Seine Estuary" --actually, in Normandy. French hedgerows are shown below. Nothing worse for attacking armies could ever be devised, with natural obstacles every 50 to 100 yards, with sheltered retreat and supply routes and little or no maneuverability possibilities.

--Photos from *29 Let's Go*

The beachhead city of Isigny (above) was blasted into rubble piles much before the 29th's 175th Regiment took it D-Plus 1 day. Below, St. Clair-sur-l'Elle, taken by the 116th's Second Battalion.

--Photos from *29 Let's Go*

Here's a typical scene as the G.I.'s fought their way through the hedgerows of Normandy. The (fox) holes at the hedgerow had taken a pounding all day, but the Americans got up and charged the next hedgerow, often no more than 100 yards away, only to repeat the action, and repeat and repeat. We called this the 100-yard dash. We were supposed to yell "Twenty-nine Let's Go", but when we did (rarely) it often became "Twenty-nine Let's Go--Home". In the photo, the U. S. Sherman tank on the right has just fired its 75mm cannon in support of the charge, but because of the *bocage* terrain cannot possibly keep up, hedgerow by hedgerow. We thought tanks drew more fire than they were worth under these circumstances.   --Photo from *29 Let's Go*

2

Back Into Bocage Country

---

*Hedgerow fighting is closely related to war in the
jungle, where see-touch, then shoot fast, is vital*

---

*M*y orders were dated, "12 August, 1944--2nd
Lieut. William F. Arendt 0-1318401 to G Company, 116th
Infantry Regiment, 2000 yards southeast of Vire, France.
princ duties Inf Unit Cmdr 15429." The number is the
M.O.S., or military specialty number. And for anyone who
carries a 1542 (Infantry Unit Leader) designation it is next
to impossible to change; some people would say
impossible.

I overheard one senior officer's comment earlier:
"Valuable people, these junior 15-42's. We lose too many
of them for no good reasons." Another observer of the U.
S. Army at war once remarked, "In infantry combat
situations be either a private or a colonel. Any rank in
between means you're out in front at least sometime."

As the lowest-ranking officer heading any army
assault group, the lieutenant platoon leader doing his job
is always forward, I found out. And, as I recall, I never
saw any rank above a first lieutenant in my operations
zone during my entire combat career.

The next day was a quiet Sunday, sparkling and a
bit too cool for my kind of August. The 29th Division
trucks picked up all of their replacement troops at the 86th

Battalion headquarters. We filled three 6-by-6 trucks, and there were two other officers and five enlisted men, including two sergeants, reporting to George Company. Others in the convoy went to different units in the regiment or division.

From our weeks together in the "repple depple", I knew slightly the others going to Company G. They included a first lieutenant, George Herrick (we called him Cowboy because he was from Wyoming) and another second looey named Tony Ceresa. Ceresa was quiet, somewhat moody. He never said much to anyone.

It was one of the replacement sergeants, a chap named Ardith Perkins, to whom I paid particular attention. Perk had a Virginia drawl and a cheerful but no-nonsense way of handling himself in what I call "heavy traffic." You could tell he was used to command situations under stress. I figured he also was one of the few original Virginians left on the Division's fighting lines. He was. He had been hit on D-Day and was just returning from the hospital. He didn't figure to see many of his old buddies.

The 29th, I learned, had taken more than 7,000 casualties, killed and wounded, since D-Day, when the 116th and the 16th Regiment of the First Division hit Omaha Beach. Any World War II infantry division that I knew about would be hard pressed to put 3,000 able-bodied front-line troops into action at any given time. Those 7,000 casualties meant replacement of the Division's fighting force more than twice in 60 days. The Blue and Gray took 2,440 casualties on D-Day, more than any other American division. Most of these came in the first hour or hour and a half.

Perk told me quietly about his D-Day experiences. He was in charge of a five-man bangalore torpedo squad. Each squad member carried a piece of the torpedo which was to be assembled at the target site or as a TNT charge. The bangalore men's duties were to rush to the barbed wire on the beach, shove the assembled, pipe-like torpedo under the wire, arm the fuse and blow a gap. Following infantry then could penetrate the wire and get to the next set of obstacles. Or they could attack a fortified position with the TNT charge people again leading the way--or start climbing Omaha Beach cliffs. It worked beautifully in months of practice in England, Perk said. But that was when no one was shooting at them.

"Nobody ever did knock out those Jerry guns on the cliffs until they ran out of ammunition," Perk claimed. "We called for smoke on them and that never happened either. It was downright weird that any of us made it."

Perk's torpedo team got split up right at the start when G Company tried to cut across 1,000 yards of direct fire impact beach to get to the company's assigned landing positions. Few of them made it. Perk himself was picked up, twice wounded in the hip and upper body, that night. He had lain in the rising tide and wet sand all day, alternately passing out and trying not to move so as not to draw more fire.

"I know what it is to die," he commented wryly.

He remembered hearing about Company A of the 116th, landing with the Rangers just to G Company's right. Alpha Company lost 96 percent of its effective strength before it could fire a shot.

Eventually demolition teams like Sergeant Perkins' and special engineer groups blew six gaps in the wire. Two of these were in the 116th area. But once through the wire, the Blue and Gray faced fortified strong points. The Germans had 12 operating at Omaha Beach, the most on any beach segment confronting the Allies. The Germans, too, realized that the Omaha attack segment offered a smooth beach capable of handling large incoming traffic volumes. This was a beach to be denied, a place where the Krauts wanted to throw the Allies back into the Channel. They almost did.

General Eisenhower, in his official report to the Combined Chiefs of Staff, explained the situation on Omaha Beach, where the entire invasion could fail or succeed by the actions of a relatively few men.

"It was in the *St. Laurent-sur-Mer* sector, on Omaha Beach, where the American V Corps assault was launched, that the greatest difficulties were experienced. Not only were the surf conditions worse than elsewhere, causing heavy losses in amphibious tanks and landing craft among the mined obstacles, but the leading formations--the 116th Infantry of the 29th Division at *Vierville-sur-Mer* and the 16th Infantry of the 1st Division at *Colleville-sur-Mer*--had the misfortune to encounter at the beach the additional strength of a German division, the 352nd Infantry, which had recently reinforced the coastal garrison.

"Against the defense offered in this sector, where the air bombing had been largely ineffective and the naval guns were hampered by the configuration of the ground, which made observation difficult, we were able to make little impression. Exhausted and disorganized at the edge of the pounding breakers, the Americans were at first pinned to the beaches but, despite a murderous fire from the German field guns along the cliffs, with extreme gallantry, they worked their way through the enemy positions. The cost was heavy; before the beaches were cleared some 800 men of the 116th had fallen, and a third of the 16th were lost, but by their unflinching courage, they turned what might have been a catastrophe into a glorious victory."

I didn't read about my new unit's D-Day heroics the night before I joined them, but I did eventually read about how the 116th, then known as the 2nd Virginia, became the backbone of Stonewall Jackson's brigade during the Civil War. They won the day for the South at the first Battle of Bull Run, or Manassas, when they "held like a stone wall" against a vastly superior Union force at Henry House Hill.[1]

During World War I, I also read, the Blue and Gray fought well in the Meuse-Argonne.[2] The 29th's battle flags were no strangers in France--for two wars.

After Omaha, the Blue and Gray were the first troops to enter St. Lo. The celebrated and saluted Major of St. Lo was Thomas Howie, Third Battalion commander from the 116th Regiment.

Vire was the next key city and road junction point, and the 29th took that too, just a week ahead of my arrival. G Company, in fact, had been the second unit into Vire. The company captured 115 prisoners in that battle as the Germans had to begin dealing with a crumbling Normandy front.

---

[1] *I Rode with Stonewall*, by Henry Kidd Douglas
[2] *Fighting Soldier*, by Joseph Douglas Lawrence

Vire formed the left shoulder of the St. Lo breakthrough. A few days before I joined them, their job in punching a hole in the German lines finally done, the 29th was relieved by the Second Infantry Division and went into a rest area to receive new equipment and replacements.

Our trip from "repple depple" to the regiment took us through St. Lo, that storied small road junction city whose capture was vital to the breakout in Normandy. Not much was left. I remember hills with piles of bricks and rubble and M.P. traffic-directed routes through the heart of the city, also framed by rubble piles. Our small convoy paused at the main town square and the still-standing spire of the Church of Notre Dame. It was here that Major Howie's flag-draped coffin rested for several days after the city fell. A sign remained at the site. It read, "Welcome to the City of St. Lo, liberated by the 29th Infantry Division on July 19, 1944. 29, Let's Go! Maj. Gen. Charles H. Gerhardt, commanding."

In truth, the 29th was not the only division to take St. Lo. The 35th Division's 134th Infantry Regiment (Nebraska National Guard origins) was on the Blue and Gray's right flank most all the way and the 2nd Division played a key role, too. I've always suspected that the dramatic General Gerhardt stage-managed a bit here, as he did by routing his new 29th Division replacements through the city for indocrination-impression purposes. Too, Major Howie never made it alive to St. Lo. He died the day before its capture; but again, General Gerhardt never missed a drumbeat to boost his division's morale. He arranged for Howie's coffin, draped with an American flag, to be displayed in the town square. The resulting publicity electrified America, creating a another "hero" to satisfy a public need in wartime.

My primary reaction to the St. Lo ruins echoed one G. I.'s opinion when he first saw it: "We sure liberated the hell out of this place."

Our replacement group was eagerly awaited, I was informed by a division driver. George Company, for example, had 81 men and one officer when we reported. Normal operating strength was around 150 men and three

Nearly all roads in bocage country were sunken death traps. When G.I.'s crossed them they did so at a gallop, and they never used them for pathways unless there was no other way. The vehicles shown here are German.
--*Photo from 29 Let's Go*

The Major of St. Lo, Tom Howie of the 116th, (insert) became a national impact event when his body was placed in the town square. Major Tom, a Virginian, was actually killed a day or so before St. Lo fell, and reportedly was not in good favor with Division at the time, but General Gerhardt wanted a symbol to dramatize the fall of the big barrier to the breakout to the 29th, even though other American units had as much right to claim St. Lo as the Blus and Gray.--*29 Let's Go*

to four officers. In those days of combat manpower shortages (they were to get much worse in a couple of months) no one paid much attention to the army's table of organization charts calling for 188 men and six officers per rifle company.

Second Lieutenant John Bookless, an earlier replacement from the Boston area, was the only officer left in Company G when we arrived. And when he saw First Lieutenant Herrick and the two of us he greeted us like long-missing Rotarian relatives.

He quickly turned over command to Herrick, introduced us around and then poured the Scotch. The 29th had been shoulder-to-shoulder with the British for several weeks and would mostly remain so during the rest of the war. Our Limey friends always had Scotch, food and excellent, even beautiful, revolvers (I believe they were Smith & Wesson) to trade for our cigarettes and food--and they actually liked our C and K rations. The English also had a fondness for the American Colt .45 automatic pistols, a ugly, heavy brute of a weapon which, while not very accurate for anything over 20 feet distant, did pack a wallop if one of its slugs ever hit a body part, no matter how remote.

Jack Bookless was, and probably still is, an unusual combination of a total party and total organization man. We drank, exchanging experiences and stories, until the light hours. Yet he gave us an accurate rundown on key noncoms, people to look to and people to look away from if something needed to be done. He outlined the company position and its strengths and weaknesses better than I could have done if I was sober, which none of us was by morning.

At one moment around midnight Bedcheck Charlie came over, and this time he dropped several sticks of anti-personnel bombs. These were not calculated to do great harm but certainly were disconcerting to any troops lying exposed in fields as most members of G Company were at the time. This was supposed to be a rest area, after all, and miles from any action.

Bookless and I scrambled in the same direction, towards an abandoned farm building with only a couple of blackened spars serving as a roof. We arrived at the door at the same time and collided sharply. Recoiling, we both sat down as the bombs whistled down. I think we realized at the same time what a ridiculous scene we were, sprawled at the front of a roofless shack which offered no protection whatsoever. I suppose the troops hearing us both roaring with laughter during a bombing raid must have thought we'd lost it.

By acclamation--and of course, seniority--Jack Bookless got the executive officer's job. That suited him fine. Never one to lead a charge, Jack liked the company command post, which generally brought up the rear with all the communications gear. Just to show fate played no favorites, however, the Book managed to get wounded and hospitalized twice before he welcomed me back to the company later that year after I was hit. There's a lesson here: There are no safe places in a front-line infantry company.

The new company commander was a reservist from Laramie, Wyoming. Tall, gangly, laconic, he suited the nickname Cowboy. He even smoked a corncob pipe. Lieutenant Herrick was a good 10 years older than the rest of his officers, although it was hard to tell how old Tony Ceresa was.

Herrick and I meshed well. He was always thoughtful and didn't mind taking a chance. He would back you if he asked you to decide, as he often did. He must have gotten a bad deal somewhere in his service history to be only a first john (1st Lieutenant) at his age. And he was not in the best position here to make it through the month, let alone to make his captain's bars.

One thing was made clear at the start of my assignment with the Blue and Gray, and I think it was at a battalion officers meeting: There will be few medals awarded, even fewer promotions (only on performance, not seniority) and, when not on the line, a parade ground mentality, including buckled chin straps on helmets, will be maintained. Our General Gerhardt was a Patton-type soldier, complete with pearl handled revolver and swagger, plus a challenging attitude, especially toward his officers.

Lieutenant Ceresa, our third second looey in G Company, always remained a mystery to me. We were not hostile, but we had no communication. Later, when we were shouting at each other, I wished I had known him better.

There was another second lieutenant, by name of Thomas Smith, who came to G Company on August 20, a week after I arrived. I must admit I simply don't remember him at all, but his name is carried in the company's morning report (a written personnel and situation report to battalion headquarters made daily) until September 1, when he is reported seriously wounded. We were under heavy mortar and artillery attack that day, I recall, and Smith must have taken some fragments. Company records show no further report on Smith; he did not rejoin the outfit while I was there, at least. I had to have met him and talked to him more than once, but his name and any memory concerning him draw blanks for me as I write this.

After our welcoming party--or maybe it was during it--I picked my sergeants for the Third Platoon. They included Perkins and another Virginian, by name Paul Edwards. I never called him anything but "Edwards" or "Sergeant", but I certainly could have called him "soldier" because he was that and more. He trained as a member of the elite provisional 29th Ranger Battalion. He had been wounded at least three times since D-Day, but here he was, coming back again. I quickly found out that whenever I wanted something even slightly risky done, I could call on Edwards. Between us, I knew we could handle the platoon, and with Perk for a dependable backup, how could we lose?

There was one other human element I really lucked out on. His name was Walter Olencki, a private, first class, from Brooklyn. Olencki joined George Company as a replacement. He was a radio operator assigned to the infantry because victory in World War II didn't require any more radio operators; it needed riflemen. I spotted him as an interesting-looking individual standing with the to-be-assigned company pool of replacements. It was just a day or two after my arrival.

I asked Olencki if he knew anything about radios--a completely blind stab on my part because I needed a radio operator. He said he did and told me about his original specialty.

I said he now was my platoon radio operator and No. 1 runner and assistant. He liked the No. 1 assistant part and took the job.

Olencki--I sometimes called him Irish for kicks and I think he kind of liked it--was a wise-cracking, smart, bouncy type of individual who always looked like he was attached to the end of a 220-volt power line. If I could keep him on the ground, I decided, I would have a valuable team member with the type of Polish joker personality every outfit involved in a serious mission really needs.

Put this type of person into a really stressful situation, which we were about to enter, and you generally end up with a superior performance by him and those around him, I've found.

The biggest problem I had in those training days following my assignment to George Company was what to do with my inherited platoon sergeant, my second in command. A tech sergeant who had the been with the company since its training days in England, he was the Regiment's light heavyweight boxing champion and he was treated with respect by all who approached, including the regimental commander. What he was doing in a rifle platoon was puzzling. He should have been in Division headquarters or in a graves registration unit.

In any event, my sergeant always disappeared when he heard incoming shelling, even in those days of defense and training near Vire. I figured he was bringing up the platoon rear, which is where he should be--or even the company rear, which is where he obviously wanted to be.

A major Company G transfusion was underway that Sunday of August. The company was the destination for another 76 replacements; they kept arriving during the day and night and into the next day. Edwards and Perkins looked over the newcomers carefully. I was sure the pick of the litter ended up in the Third Platoon's area. At any rate, we filled out first with around 35 men total, less than 10 of whom had ever been shot at. These virgins included their lieutenant.

Pursuing the retreating Germans became a game after the St. Lo breakthrough. We would hit opposition every afternoon or early evening, deploy our units and attack the next morning. Nothing was there by then, and this process of controlled German retreat would be repeated daily.

--Map from *29 Let's Go*

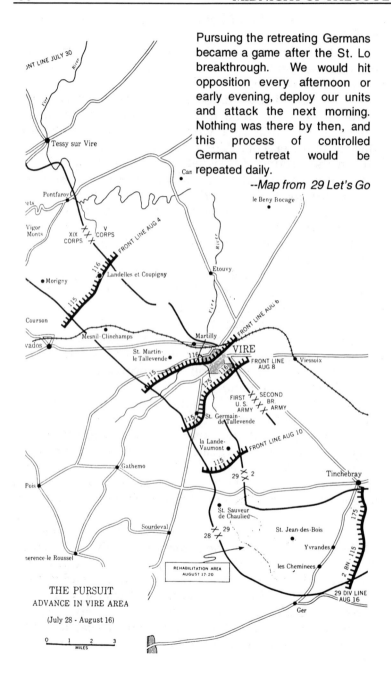

THE PURSUIT
ADVANCE IN VIRE AREA

(July 28 - August 16)

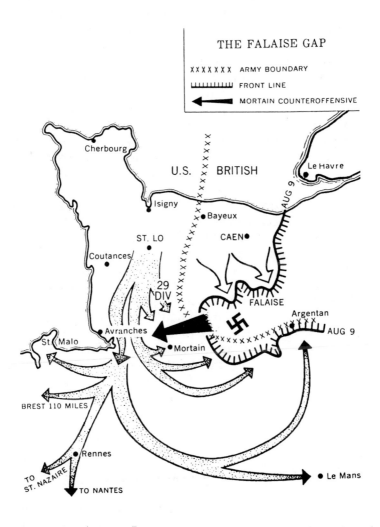

THE FALAISE GAP

XXXXXX ARMY BOUNDARY
⊥⊥⊥⊥⊥⊥⊥⊥ FRONT LINE
◄ MORTAIN COUNTEROFFENSIVE

Brunt of the German counteroffensive at Mortain fell on one of the 29th's neighbors, the Old Hickory Division (30th) of North Carolina. Close-in air power, for one of its firsts, played a decisive role in stopping the last major German effort before the wholesale retreat to the Fatherland began. The Allies never closed the Falaise Gap, reportedly because of a turf war between Montgomery and Patton.

--Map from *29 Let's Go*

The regiment, now the 116th Regimental Combat Team and designated First Army reserve, remained in a rest area only until Wednesday, the 16th, when we were trucked to a defensive position near Yvrandes and Tinchebray. We took over the entire division's front while our two sister regiments, the 115th and the 175th, re-outfitted themselves in our old rest area.

I dimly remembered something about Tinchebray from my European history courses which I took, it seemed, a couple of centuries ago. Tinchebray, an English name, was not so strange to find in Normandy, I realized. This country was owned by England for nearly 100 years around the 12th century. English kings then were mostly Frenchmen from Normandy, following William the Conqueror's successful invasion of England in 1066 A. D.

Later, in an Army hospital in England, I looked up Tinchebray. There was a battle in 1106 A.D. when Robert Curthose, William's son, returned from a Crusade to find Henri Beauclerc, a half brother, had become King Henry I of England and claimed Normandy as part of England. Henry defeated Robert at the Battle of Tinchebray and had him imprisoned until his death 28 years later. In the meantime, and for another 80 years, England ruled Normandy. In 1259, the treaty following the lengthy religious wars between France and England gave Normandy back to France. Thus our Normandy invasion was actually a homecoming for the English.

Our position near Tinchebray in 1944 A. D. was a defensive stance in name only, because the closest German had to have been scurrying away from us at least six miles to the east.

We sent out contact patrols--in fact, I headed one of the first--only to discover that we had elements of the British 3rd Division in front of us. Our front had been pinched out by the closing elements of the Falaise Pocket. This presaged the end of the Seventh German Army which opposed us all through Normandy, and it precipitated the Allies' headlong dash to Paris and to Germany.

In the war or not, the Blue and Gray did not rest. Our general was never one to let things idle. We began intensive hedgerow attack training, to the dismay of all. Why, we asked, were we going back over what we had already done? We were leaving the Normandy *bocage* country at last, we thought. Nevertheless we continued pitching ourselves over the tops of hedgerows, free-falling down the other side, getting up and running as fast as we could to the next sheltering hedgerow, all the time yelling "29--Let's Go!" We even had an area where we could fire our weapons as we ran. This was hard work, but we did it and not with smiles.

A couple of days later we began close order drill in Norman farm fields. Now this was odd, too, but our pleasant and unrealistic anticipation that we could be marching in the Paris victory parade came with the drills. So they weren't so bad.

Within two days we knew the answers. By August 22 we would be leaving for the fortress city of Brest on the westernmost coast of France, the Brittany Peninsula, to take control of that important port and potential major supply city. Three bloodied and veteran divisions of the First Army, the 2nd, 8th and 29th, would form an assault force under VIII Corps to do the job, and it must be done in a particular hurry. Again, through the hated hedgerows.

Brest was actually one of the goals of the breakout, and Prime Minister Winston Churchill of Great Britain wanted it badly.[1] His idea was to push the battle in Italy and continue the main battle against the Germans in France. For this he would need a major port. He did not anticipate the collapse of the German Seventh Army in Normandy, nor was he in favor of the invasion of Southern France called Operation Dragoon. He actually wanted a Balkans invasion to forestall any Russian move in that area, what he called the "soft underbelly of Europe."

In any event, the Allied command gambled that its forces could seize Brest quickly and had sent the 6th Armored Division into Brittany to collect the German surrender notices.

When we were briefed by intelligence people, we were told that we probably need only to show up to induce a rapid German surrender. Yes, they did mention

---

[1] *Delivered from Evil*, by Robert Leckie, Harper & Row

that Major General Hermann Ramcke and his parachute regiments of Italy's Monte Cassino resistance fame had taken over the Brest area defenses and that several thousand submarine and navy personnel located in Brittany were likely to join the paratroopers; but, they asked, who could stop us? These Germans were people without a cause, isolated, starving and nowhere near the Fatherland as it was about to be invaded. How wrong they were!

By this time I had come to recognize the worth of the Blue and Gray, particularly the Gray as it applied to my Virginia men. These people were shot up, injured, but back they came to the old outfit, and I felt they really wanted to.

Less than a third of my guys were from Virginia, but theirs was the third I depended upon. In those few training days we had together I tried hard to meld an outfit around them. First, I did everything everybody else did, including running the General Gerhardt sprint from hedgerow to hedgerow. Second, I took time to bullshit with anybody who would talk to me and some who wouldn't, and third, I asked advice even if I had already mostly made up my mind.

I tried to bring that elusive "unit think" approach to platoon operations. This meant individuals thinking of the group's welfare and safety before their own--actually a very difficult task but an essential one in any combat team effort. And I think I was at least partially successful in our Normandy training.

In my opinion, hedgerow fighting is the toughest in the world, with the possible exception of close-contact jungle warfare. Traditionally, the attacker needs a 3 to 1 advantage; the Germans showed they could defend successfully in the Normandy *bocage* country against a 5 to 1 ratio, and the reasons are simple: Each hedgerow is easily defended; hedgerows running at right angles to the line of attack offer good retreating shelter to where another defense line can be set up, sometimes even at the next hedgerow; heavy equipment, such as tanks, are virtually useless and artillery is handicapped because of the closeness of the fighting troops. In Normandy we were fighting for 100 yards at a time. It was World War I trench warfare all over again, 26 years later.

I believe our biggest disappointment in our assignment to take Brest was not the fact that we would miss Paris and the open country after Normandy (although both of these mattered greatly to our experienced solders who had seen more than their share of close quarter assaults and killing). It was primarily the fact that we would be returning--or in fact, never leaving--hedgerow country. And hedgerows in Brittany were even thicker and higher than those in Normandy, we were told. That was one thing our intelligence got right--they were.

But my men were ready, I believed. Whatever happens, we were eager. In more serious moments, I wondered how long the platoon would stay in "unit-think". I wanted it to last forever. The unit feeling is indescribable to someone who has not been a member or leader of a team poised for action--but it is one of the greatest rewards in life, particularly when one realizes its transitory nature. I've often thought that my days preparing the platoon for combat were similar to those of a football or basketball coach with faith in his team. I knew and loved every one of those guys in my platoon and knew they would perform.

We all realized that a few days in combat could change everything, and I knew that the sole proof of our worth, sad as it seems in reflection, would come in combat where people get killed. That's exactly where we were headed.

3

Fight for a Fortress City

*My first killing was part of a shooting frenzy
for which I wasn't proud.*

Sunday, just a week after I joined G Company, we were packing for a big move. We took what a soldier could carry, no more. And a lot of us chose to carry the minimum--the clothes on our back, our toilet articles, a spare ration or two, some writing materials with a couple of photos and letters, maybe a souvenir, plus what I called a secret backscratcher. That's anything which creates personal enjoyment--a deck of cards, a sexy pinup picture, an extra goodie or a bottle of old and rare. My particular backscratcher was doubled, a bottle of Scotch and a couple of books--almost any written word on nearly any subject would do. The Scotch either came from our monthly ration of booze (yes, the Army thought of everything in those days, including free cigarettes to front line troops) or from our trades with the Brits--I don't remember which.

Word came down before evening chow that we should rest lightly that night, and sure enough, the following morning at 4:30 we were shook awake and told we were boarding trucks in an hour. A hot meal was waiting.

Sorting out people and equipment in the darkness, even if it involves a disciplined group, is a frustrating task. I always felt like a cub scout den mother at these times. Something invariably was lost or went wrong--and just as invariably turned out to be nothing critical.

So it was this time. Somebody had made off with my bedroll while I was chowing down. I didn't have time to look for it; I just hoped it would show up later when we hit our next rest area. I never did see that bedroll again, but then I didn't make it to the next company rest area either. Eventually, four or five months later, I believe I got parts of what was in the bedroll back, including some dress uniforms I needed badly. No pistols, Brit bottles, books or souvenirs--all of which I had painfully bargained for.

When everybody in the platoon was loaded--into two trucks for this trip--I hopped into the front seat of the lead company truck and we rolled.

And how we rolled. Until that morning I'd never ridden so fast in a truck, let alone in a dirt-caked, creaking Army rustbuggy with cast-iron seats and a wild man at the wheel. I remember being waved through what must have been high traffic intersections with never a slackening of speed. If our guys, bouncing in the back end of the truck, didn't understand the urgency of our mission before, they did after a few minutes into that ride.

Military Police were on practically every corner as we zoomed past Avranches and slowed for Mont St. Michel, that famous monastery island jutting from the sea.

I remember we all stopped after dawn for some obvious relief reasons, and we all got a good look at the island abbey, probably at low tide. There was this never-ending sandbar connecting the majestic island's seemingly sheer walls to the mainland. The sun, coming up behind us, painted the island and the sand a glorious yellow and red gold. Low tide pools of water sparkled like jewels. Here was a sublimely paradoxical moment that I'll always carry with me--the scene of heavily-armed fighting men relieving themselves while standing and looking up to this triumph of religious sacrifice and dedication. I did not, at the time or since, consider it sacrilegious. It was just an intriguing moment of pause in a world of violence.

A month later I looked up Mont St. Michel in a library near my hospital in England. I learned that the cathedral was built during the eighth century on a rock rising from the Gulf of St. Malo. The rock had been a shrine long before the Christians came to France, but it was said that it became a chapel of prayer

Mont Saint-Michel, a spiritual event even from a distance--and a beauty moment to balance war's ugliness.

when the Bishop of Avranches had a vision of the Archangel St. Michael asking that a chapel for him be built on the scene. The Bishop then awoke, thinking he was dreaming, and did nothing.

Another time and at a later date, St. Michael appeared to him in a dream-like sequence and, again he did nothing. The third time, St. Michael demanded that the chapel be built in his honor and, to punctuate his request, he vigorously punched the Bishop in the head with his forefinger. Contemporaries of the Bishop reported that his skull always carried St. Michael's finger indentation.

In any event, the Bishop built the chapel, finally, and Mont St. Michel later became a Benedictine Abbey with a church whose foundations were 73 meters above sea level, seemingly balanced on top of a slim rock jutting from the sea bed.

Stendahl described it as "an equilateral triangle of increasingly brilliant red verging on rose and standing out against a background of gray."

To me, that particular morning, it looked like a giant finger pointing to the sky. I took it as a symbol of hope. No prayer, but a lot of reflective thought from me.

Tragically, it seems we never find time to get back to some of the memorable scenes of our past. I never got back to Mont St. Michel, but I'll never forget that precious moment of sublime understanding and peace.

Our roll through Brittany took nearly 12 hours. It wasn't the convoy's fault. Whenever we were clear of villages and people, drivers put pedals to the floor. The problems came when we approached villages. The entire population was in the streets, cheering, waving bottles of champagne and wine, throwing flowers and food, asking or wanting to trade for *l'essence* (gasoline), laughing, singing, having one big liberation party. And there we were, their liberators, the objects of their gratitude, riding through. It's a wonder we ever got to Brest!

Frankly, we loved it. Soldiers never see enough triumphal marches. In Rome, emperors lived (and died) for them.

Ours was truly an historical moment--not so noted in WWII history books. No welcome march in Paris could equal this reception. I finally climbed into the back of the truck because that's where all the action was. For sure, we couldn't take any Bretons, including their young girls, along with us. That forcible separating of girls and G. I.'s got to be part of my job, all done with a great deal of laughter. My platoon knew how far they could go.

Maybe it was the times; certainly it was the place and the people. Americans have no way of understanding the emotions released by masses of people after enduring four or five years of actual scratching in the dirt for a bare existence under the gross whims of disciplinarian conquerors. We were dealing with emotions at flood tide.

During the occupation the average French city housewife stood in the ration line for hours for her ersatz coffee, a few vegetables and potatoes, meat on rare occasions, no fruit. When it could be found, ersatz soap made of ground horse chestnuts and slaked lime was a true treasure. Before the Liberation, advertisements such as this appeared in at least one Parisian newspaper:

<u>Cat Eaters, Attention!</u>
During the present period of shortages
Certain hungry people are not afraid
to trap cats to make a nice stew
of them. These people do not know
the danger which threatens them.
In fact, cats which serve a useful purpose
in killing and eating rats which carry the
most dangerous germs can, because of the
fact, be particularly harmful when eaten.[1]

French farmers, of course, did much better than city dwellers during those years. The farmers of Normandy and Brittany were visited regularly by black marketers and by hungry city people who were ready to pay almost anything to get food. New fortunes were made in the midst of deprivation.

Even with this history of haves and have-nots of a bitter, four-year occupation, I've never imagined such a joyous, spontaneous welcome celebration as the people of Brittany showed us as we rode through their country. Flags were everywhere. Wine flowed. V-signs and tears, laughter and screams. As I recall, our convoy went through no large towns. But then again, Brittany was mostly farm, with plenty of beautiful greenery and with a few large coastal cities. The

---

[1] *The French Against the French,* by Milton Dank, J.B. Lippincott & Co.

country was largely untouched by the war physically, had never seen large German troop concentrations and, with the exception of the Atlantic submarine ports on its southern shoreline, were victims of isolation rather than violation.

A week or two earlier, following the St. Lo breakout, the Sixth Armored Division hustled to Brittany in an effort to take the westernmost province without a fight. The Sixth was generally successful, with the exception of St. Nazaire, Lorient and Brest, all submarine ports and all defended. The retreating German Second Parachute Regiment, plus supporting units, hightailed it to Brest from Normandy, barely arriving before the Sixth Armored. Then the parachutists organized defenses to include German marines, navy personnel and coast artillery garrison soldiers. The submariners made good ground fighters.

To coordinate defenses for what was now a major enemy force behind Allied lines, Hitler appointed Major General Hermann Ramcke, a paratroop fanatic who promised Hitler he would hold Brest for three months, and in any case, leave an unusable wreckage of a port behind him.

On its hurried way to the west tip of Brittany, the Sixth Armored was mistakenly diverted to the ports of St. Malo and Dinard (reportedly causing a verbal explosion from General Patton who, correctly, wanted to beat Ramcke to Brest), but managed to reach the submarine base area by August 7, where it hit resistance seven miles north of the city. A surrender message was sent. General Ramcke declined, and the battle was on.

French Maquis members, strong in the region, told us that had the Sixth Armored been able to attack the city two days earlier, they might have taken it without a big fight. But our people doubted this. Brest even then had at least 35,000 Germans, mostly unorganized, but more than twice the force of the entire Sixth Armored.

Here's what the official history of the 29th Division said about Brest:

"The defenses of Brest had been constructed to withstand attack by land or sea. For miles beyond the city hedgerows had been prepared for the expected (Allied) offensive. An outer band of defenses consisted of an abundance of strong points, heavy in automatic weapons and self-propelled guns, dug well into the earth, some fortified with concrete and steel, all of them forming a great defensive arc that swept around the city.

"An inner band of ramparts was modernized with steel pillboxes, antitank ditches, road barriers and minefields. Within months of preparation, these positions had become the ultimate in defense. . . According to G-2 (Army Group intelligence section) estimates, this fortress area held approximately 20,000 enemy. Actually, the Brest garrison (when it surrendered after sustaining huge losses) comprised nearly 50,000."

The 116th Regimental Combat Team (RCT), the advance party for the Division, pulled into an area south of Ploudalmezeau at 1900 hours that evening. We were on combat status, and set up a perimeter defense approximately 10 miles northwest of Brest. We sent out patrols immediately, mostly to determine if other 29th Division unit debarking and assembly areas were secure.

Our first contacts with the Germans from these patrols were on the far side of the town of St. Renan, about five miles from Brest. Our Third Battalion stayed in contact with Jerry while the rest of the division unloaded and moved directly into lines of attack.

Our division was positioned to move from west to east, along the coast. The 8th Division was to attack from north to south and the 2nd Division from east to west. Because the entire Brest campaign was priority, we had all the pledged artillery and air support we could use, but it didn't work out that way. Our supporting artillery often ran out of ammunition because the entire European theater couldn't deliver enough shells, supplies and gasoline in those days. Hence, our quest for a major seaport and supply depot became even more important--and conversely, more elusive.

To our right, charged with reducing coastal gun emplacements and four forts, was the Fifth Ranger Battalion. I took one of the first patrols in that direction and found nothing other than the still-active forts. Their defenders let us have it, long range, when we poked our heads over the hedgerows to look at them. At the rate they were firing at 10 men, I figured they had plenty of ammunition and plenty of fight. The Rangers probably were right not to be there yet, I reported to headquarters later.

The next day we moved with the 115th into an attack formation southeast of St. Renan. We crossed the line of departure just after noon and, in a column of battalions, the 116th moved several thousand yards to near the town of Guilers, less than four miles from the Brest city limits. The Second Battalion, mine, was last in line, in reserve, and the Third Battalion led the assault. It began meeting heavy resistance towards darkness.

Our battalion took moderate to heavy shelling most of the day, a condition I've found most troops in reserve generally inherit. Battalion reserve units are maybe 200 to 500 yards back of the front lines, and the enemy is never sure at any given moment where, exactly, the attack lines are; so they target most of their shelling areas a couple of hundred yards behind the contact points, back to where they think most of the enemy is. This also assures them that they're not blasting their own defense.

There's really nothing a soldier can do about this beating from a distance. He is in a column and he must stay in place. I figure there are three actions possible: Dig a hole if the stop is for more than a minute or two (if in doubt, dig!); pray a lot, or realize that if you're going to get hit, you will get hit--be a fatalist. Maybe it takes all three.

I chose the latter course. I stood up and walked around during many of these shellings, talking to the men. I wasn't trying to be a hero or set false standards, truly. Some of them may have thought I was crazy. But I believe more of them appreciated my moves. In any event, my actions seemed to give them some sense of security, and since I didn't get hit, I must have messaged to them that maybe this wasn't so bad after all.

There was also stark terror on my part several times while under artillery attack. I remember one day where we were caught in an open field, first by ak-ak (anti-aircraft) guns to our right, then by a heavy piece firing air bursts. Then both together. There is nothing more terrifying to a grunt soldier than artillery air bursts, unless it's an enemy flame-thrower within 30 yards-- or, as I was to find out later--an unmarked minefield.

I remember that 10 minutes under shelling bursting 20 to 30 feet overhead, hearing metal shards zinging and zooming past, hearing the yells and screams of the wounded and being able to do nothing. Finally I came to believe that there was a

A pause between hedgerows. The G. I.'s will climb that hedgerow in front of them, lunging to the exposed side, and then run in a skirmish line to the next obstacle. They'll follow their artillery as closely as possible (often within 100 yards) hopefully to catch the Germans with their heads down.   --29 Let's Go!

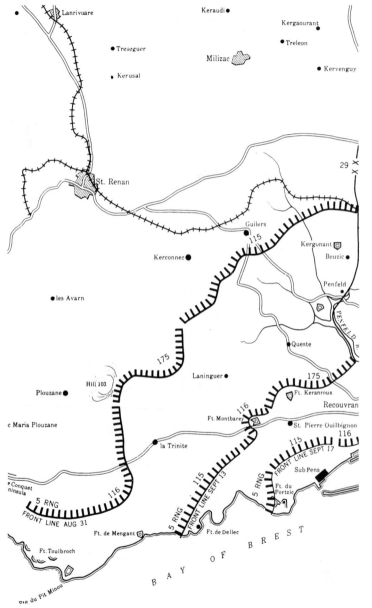

Mapmakers like to draw neat, complete lines. And so it was with our attack positions on the City of Brest. There were no Allied troops, except my platoon and the Fifth Rangers, between La Trinite and the coast from late August through mid-September, 1944. And note the burp in the lines around Fort Montbarey. It held the entry key to Brest from the west and drew all of our attention. *--Map from 29 Let's Go*

higher fate which had life or death in hand, dealing one person a lucky card and another an unlucky one.

In the meantime, my nose was digging into the ground--and I really prayed then! It seemed as if I was lying naked in the middle of a field while dozens of people at point blank range were throwing rocks at me.

Artillery always brought terror and death from far away and this seemed much more ghastly to me than death delivery systems coming from people one could see and do something about. We lost considerable numbers of men that day but I was untouched. I began to feel I could survive anything in this war--truly, a breezy combat high began about that time. It ended just a few days later after I had replaced a large portion of the platoon twice.

By Saturday night, two days later, the Division had decided on an end-around play for the 116th. We left our portion of the front to the 115th and swung around to the coastal road on the right of the 175th to attack down the main Le Conquet-Brest Highway, a natural ridge line paralleling the coast and leading directly to Recouvrance, a Brest suburb just north of the submarine pens.

Unless the Rangers were there, we still had an exposed flank on our right to the sea--but we made excellent progress with our Second Battalion in the regimental attack lead. It was a punchy, straight, frontal infantry attack with troops closely following their moving artillery fire zones. By eight o'clock Monday morning we had covered two miles, taken all of our objectives and suffered only minor casualties.

Again, I had that untouchable, God-like feeling; there is no way to describe the inner strengths and feelings uncovered through leadership of men in combat. I still remember--50-plus years later--those supreme moments of triumph in war.

But the next day was a different story. The Germans had found our end run threat and moved to cover it.

The entire battalion inched forward a few hedgerows, but did not reach our objectives and came under heavy fire. We were in a column of companies, George bringing up the rear as Second Battalion reserve. The order was passed to dig in for a defensive stay that evening. George Company went into a perimeter defense on the battalion's right, and unprotected, flank.

I remember drawing another patrol the following morning in an effort to find the Rangers. After a morning's cautious advance, we finally spotted them, cooking and relaxing, in a half-cave, half-crevice hideout in the cliffs overlooking the Bay of Brest on the direct sea route to the port city's submarine pens. The Rangers were about a half-mile to our right and at least a 1,000 yards to our rear.

Their lagging didn't seem to bother them; they were interested in where we were, but only to mark it on their maps. Their charts showed three forts along the coast remaining between them and the submarine pens. They had taken one fortified gun emplacement with its supporting troops surrendering and believed they had the formula to take the others.

"You call for an air strike," one Ranger captain explained to me. "And you watch as the P-47's peel off and drop their 500-pounders. It's a pretty sight. Makes you want to sign up for the Air Corps.

"You move up while the bombing is going on. When it's over, you stand up, wave a white flag and the Germans all come out with their hands behind their heads. We got 84 prisoners already and we just started."

He allowed as how his coastal gunner prisoners probably weren't as motivated as the marines and paratroopers we were running into. But I did like his comment about the Air Corps. He was peeling a potato as he said it and commented how he wouldn't be doing this sort of thing either if he was a flyboy.

I got along well with these Rangers, sometimes considered undisciplined misfits. Maybe I wanted to be like them, seemingly uncaring and laughing, and yet taking their objectives fast and with precision. I remember Ranger Captain George Whittington's comment on leading troops: "You saw what happened on that goddamned beach (Omaha). Now you tell me how in hell you lead men from behind them."[1]

We stayed that night with the Rangers. It was party time. They even had a couple of local mademoiselles, several dogs, chickens and a pig they had picked up along the way. One

---

[1] D-Day, June 6, 1944: The Climactic Battle of the 2nd World War, by Stephen E. Ambrose, Simon & Schuster

of them told me a great story (It may be only that. I heard more recently that the same story was part of an earlier group's experience in the area):[2] Anyway, here it is:

The Germans had a fort or two on the tip of the Le Conquet Peninsula, which ships had to pass before they could enter Brest harbor. Every day the Heini Brest garrison would send the Le Conquet forces food and wine rations. The Rangers would intercept these, and would buy off one or two of the delivery party with American cigarettes, tell them to go back to Brest and say everything went well. Sure enough, the next day another delivery party was sent and duly intercepted. This went on for the better part of a week, the Ranger told me, before the Germans caught on. That's probably why they were a bit tardy in catching up with the attack, he added.

I went back to George Company convinced that the Rangers may never protect our flank, but, I predicted, they would get those forts.

We remained in defensive positions that day, preparing for a frontal attack astride the Le Conquet-Brest highway the next day. My platoon would lead George Company with Fox Company on our left, nobody on our right. The battalion was to follow, astride the highway.

We were on the lip of a downslope of hedgerow country, leading to the tiny town of La Trinite sitting close to the bottom of the bowl, a mile or so ahead. In other days La Trinite would have been a welcome sight, but now most of its red roofs were gone, along with the buildings they topped. Still visible in the evening haze were the neat green hedges, even an unplundered garden or two, plus grazing cows. But everything was deserted. Even the large sign, La Brassiere, hung at an angle over the town's former beer joint. I wondered if the Krauts had drunk all the beer.

From La Trinite, it was upward another 3,000 yards to Fort Montbarey, our ultimate objective. By now we were well into the German fortification system. Soon we would be at its heart.

Our first day as George Company's leading attack unit went well. I was happy--and I believe my platoon was even grateful--to be out of the "behind-the-lines-getting-all-the-shelling" position that we hoped we would never become too

---

[2] 29. *Let's Go*, by Joseph Ewing, Infantry Journal Press

accustomed to. Better to be moving on the attack lines, we reasoned.

We followed our artillery, primarily by just one hedgerow. We piled over the hedgerow even as shells were falling less than 100 yards ahead of us and ran for the shelter of the next hedgerow buffer. We moved several hundred yards in this manner when we were called to halt. The lines had been straightened, Lieutenant Herrick messaged, and so dig in Third Platoon, and wait until tomorrow.

I learned later that 2nd Lieut. Thomas Smith was seriously wounded that day by Jerry artillery. He had been with the company exactly 12 days. At any rate, he was now gone and, I heard, Tech Sergeant Wilson Carr, a Virginian, had command of his platoon.

One thing Division did encourage: Battlefield commissions. I knew of at least two sergeants in the 116th who became overnight second lieutenants because of their leadership abilities (they generally were transferred to other rifle companies after their promotions in order to give the platoons and the new officers fresh starts). I hoped Sergeant Carr got the chance, too, if he wanted it.

My platoon was now down to less than 20 men, but after replacements we were still the strongest in the company. We figured we'd be out in front again.

But there was quiet on the next day and the next day. Defensive positions, Battalion called it. At intervals, the German shelled us well, to the point where I started jumping into holes. More important, I was uneasy about our right flank, still open. And there remained another thousand or more yards to the coast which, I figured, was really no man's land.

I actually asked Herrick, our cowboy commander, if I could take a small patrol to the coast to see if any Rangers were around and what, if anything, was on our right flank. This I did for a few reasons, the first of which is that I was being challenged by a short redhead in my platoon to go with him on nightly "killing missions" on that flank. He did this himself, he said, and bragged that he had killed several Krauts over the last two or three nights. He knifed them in their holes while they were sleeping, he said.

That's all we ever had, his word. When I doubted his tales, he urged me to come with him, and this he said in front of several platoon members. I felt I had no choice but to accept his challenge. But I kicked myself for getting into the situation, even though I figured there were few, if any, Germans in the area.

The second reason is that I wanted to know what happened to my friends, the Fifth Rangers. Did they still have their girls? Or at least a few goodies left?

So this redheaded firebrand and I, just the two of us, went for the coast that evening. We were to be back by dark, a good four hours away, so there was no great danger or need for force. Shorty and I did a few two-man approaches (one moves, the other covers, and then alternately) on suspected German holes and fortifications, but found nothing and we eventually ended at the sea. We did run into a Ranger scout who actually shot at us, and then hollered, "Hey, I'm sorry. What are you doing up here?"

I knew the man slightly, or at least had seen him before, and he, me. So we talked a bit, found out that the Ranger fort-taking formula was still working (another two down in three days) and left with promises that he would ask his platoon leader to send a scout team our way in the next 24 hours.

"We want to know if you're still over here," I said, adding that our people were concerned about our exposed right flank.

Shorty was somewhat subdued when we got back, although I'm sure he multiplied our actions when I left the scene. I never had trouble with him again, however. And he was always ready for scout and point duty, probably the most dangerous jobs in a rifle platoon. It's actually good to have an individual like Shorty (I can't remember his real name) in a combat group even though his tall-tale type can be a pain.

The next day, September 3, was a Wednesday and a day where we very nearly spent all our manpower resources. We were back on the attack, with La Trinite heavy in our sights. The Third Platoon, again, was leading the way somewhat downhill, and this time we were making progress. We negotiated the first half dozen hedgerows right behind our artillery, screaming "29 Let's Go--(or something like fuck 29)"--all the way.

We took a dozen or more prisoners, but they weren't paratroopers. Paratroopers, we learned, we mostly had to kill to get past.

In fact, we caught six or seven of them in the open one time that afternoon. They were moving from our right, trying to set up a resistance point more to our front since we had by-passed them. We were two hedgerows away, and my platoon had perfect visibility. We opened up, me included, and we downed all of them. Even shot some of them as they were trying to get to their feet after an initial wound.

It was my first personal killing and I really wasn't proud of it. My platoon, I realized later, was in a shooting frenzy. And these were normal, apple-pie Americans I had helped train--but certainly not, I belatedly thought, to become crazy, laughing, shrieking killers. They were that day. And so was I.

It wasn't something I agonized about, but I did feel some remorse. The American Army grudgingly admired Jerry paratroops. They were good soldiers, fought fairly and, according to rumor, were professional when they took prisoners. Maybe that made me feel worse about the shooting of helpless men. It still bothers me to this day that I didn't stop the, well, massacre. Some of those people were just lying there, dying and wounded. Especially, I wonder today, was that what we were truly like then? Maniac killers? No better than the people we were fighting? I'm sure I've softened in the 50 years since that time. I know I didn't grieve for the dead Heinis then, but rather was happy we got them.

George Company had moved to the outskirts of La Trinite, where we stopped because we were at least two or three hedgerows ahead of our left flank, F Company. And we had no protection on our right, from where we immediately began to take accurate sniper fire.

The 116th Regiment's Cannon Company was in close support all the way through the Brest Campaign. Here we see it in action backing our attack in the La Trinite sector. Occasionally we had air support liaison at the battalion level, but most always had artillery forward observers with our advance companies.

--Photo from *29 Let's Go!*

4

Night Attack

*Saved by a Russian in a German uniform? That's likely a
true story of my assault on an enemy machine gun
in the middle of a silent, moonless night*

When he is stopped as an advance element in any
attack, the experienced infantryman wastes no time getting
out his shovel, officially known as an entrenching tool.
And his digging starts almost as an automatic reaction to
hitting the ground. At least that's the way it should be. In
practice, American troops didn't dig that well.

Third Platoon members on that late afternoon in
early September knew we were stopped for more than a
few minutes. So they began digging without my urging
and particularly when they saw Olencki and me attacking
the ground with our shovels.

We all were stopped--not by the Germans but
because we outran our own left flank. Plus the fact that we
had an open right flank. We were vulnerable from three
sides. The only solution was to dig for protection.

The platoon was in a two-hedgerow wide front,
with the left section hugging the Le Conquet-Brest road.
Sergeant Perkins, Olencki and I were with the right group
with five or six men. There was a young, low-lying
hedgerow between us and the left element, led by Sergeant
Edwards. Between us and along that low hedgerow

running parallel to our line of attack, the company's weapons platoon was racing to set up their light machine guns on our forward line.

After signaling a stop, I told my group I was going back to talk with Lieutenant Herrick. Automatically, Perkins knew he was in charge and Olencki knew he was digging a hole for both of us.

I didn't see any Germans anywhere. We had overrun several of their positions earlier and taken a much smaller number of prisoners than previously. That should have told us the Heinis were pulling back and regrouping on the other side of La Trinite, automatically giving us the town or what was left of it.

There didn't seem to be much opposition ahead of us. La Trinite appeared deserted. But I knew we had to wait for Fox Company on our left to catch up before we went any further. It was quiet then, but I fully expected a counterattack. Before I left I moved my automatic rifle team to our front and right.

I was in a crouched run to the rear when I heard the first sharp crack of the sniper's rifle. I hit the ground about the same time I heard Sergeant Marcum scream. He was in charge of setting up our automatic weapons along our front. I then saw him go down, doubled up and writhing and evidently belly-wounded. There's nothing worse than a gut wound. Everybody within hearing dies a little bit each time the wounded yells his pain. No one can do anything for the wound either. Marcum had to wait until the aid team could reach him and get him to medical care.

So I focused on getting back to the Company. I raised myself and dashed for the hedgerow behind us, the one we had just left. The Company's forward command should be there, or they should know where Lieutenant Herrick could be located.

I vaulted over the hedgerow into Lieutenant Ceresa's platoon, then in Company reserve. Herrick, I was informed, was on his way up.

By this time an aid man had reached Marcum and his loud groans quieted. Then I heard another crack.

John, one of my automatic riflemen, jerked and rolled over as I turned to watch. He probably was wounded only slightly because he crab-scurried back to his hole as fast as I've ever seen anyone in a prone position move. Perkins ran over to John and stayed at the hole.

By now I was looking around to try to find the sniper. No luck. The Germans gave their unseen killers smokeless powder and it was almost impossible to tell their locations without somebody to help in the triangularization process necessary. I was convinced the shots came from our right rear and fairly close, but I couldn't be positive.

As I was watching another round came from the sniper. Olencki was his target this time. When I saw Irish slump in our shallow hole, I starting running towards him. I hugged the hedgerow to my right, again in a fast-run crouch. I reached Olencki just as he was passing out. He mumbled something I couldn't understand and then, silently with his mouth and eyes open, he was basically gone. He died in my arms, his blood from a back wound surging all over the freshly dug dirt from the hole and saturating my jacket's left sleeve.

The Kraut bullet must have hit his spinal column. I couldn't feel anything in his neck arteries or pulse and I finally laid him down, picked up his radio and ran over to Perkins.

"Everybody stays down. Watch for any counter, but don't move around. I'll be back!" And as an after-thought, I handed him Olencki's radio. "Tell that fucking cowboy to get up here," I shouted. I was feeling Olencki's and Marcum's pain, plus my own frustrations, by now.

I figured I would get the First Platoon under Lieutenant Ceresa to sweep to the right and pick up the sniper. But when I reached the safety hedgerow, I found Ceresa's men talking and joking and apparently unknowing and uncaring of what was happening just 50 to 70 yards away. I found Ceresa and told him to get his men over to our right, that we were being chewed up by a sniper or snipers and needed help right now.

He did nothing but look at me, repeating the message that Herrick was on his way up. By this time, I was blowing my stack. I grabbed a G.I. by the arm and told him in no uncertain terms to "Bring Lieutenant Herrick here on the double. We have a real problem!" I confess I was ready then to put a gun on Ceresa to get him to move.

Herrick finally arrived--actually it was probably moments later-- and I told him what had happened as best I could. I volunteered to take a group around the right flank and look for the snipers. And I accused Ceresa, in not too gentle terms, of not wanting to move. Herrick and Ceresa began talking to one side. I took off again for my platoon, still cursing and shouting to anyone who would listen: "Get some men into that field--we're getting the shit knocked out of us!"

Perkins was still holding strong. No movement in front, he said. I told him help for the sniper was on its way--I didn't say I wasn't sure it really was. And as we talked, the sniper became active again, keeping us down with shots every minute or two. At the time I didn't think he was hitting anything, but I later found out he did manage to wound another Third Platoon member, plus a couple of weapons people. Sergeant Edwards' left-side Platoon section was not affected, which surely proved the shots were coming from our right rear.

By this time a stretcher team from battalion had arrived to pick up Sergeant Marcum. They calmly loaded him on a stretcher, standing all the time in full view of the sniper, and then slowly carried him away. That, for me, was true heroism.

As I look back with less emotion, it is possible the sniper did not fire at the stretcher bearers out of respect for their job. Today, I would like to believe that.

Fox Company came up on line while I was with Perk. The Second Battalion now had a solid front overlooking La Trinite. And the sniper had evidently quit. I was still seething when I returned to the Company command post. This time we got something done, anyway.

I can't remember whether or not Lieutenant Ceresa was with us when we made that right flank sweep with members of the First Platoon, but I know I was. We were a half hour or more too late. Jerry had left only an elaborate dugout with slit trench connections to the next field on the right. The sniper fire came mostly through a hedgerow gap, but the Germans were generally on higher ground and could look down our backs as they got on top of their hedgerows.

Our attack was damned unlucky, I reasoned. We missed the one field that did us any damage and the company didn't react fast enough when the enemy started shooting.

The day ended with emptiness. We had reached our objective. We had no losses until the sniper found us vulnerable. We lost good, experienced men. Irreplaceable. We, at least I, learned something about being too aggressive, sticking out too far ahead of the main body.

Mostly I learned not to expect help. I was too bitter to lament, too busy to grieve because of Olencki. I actually blamed myself for becoming too close to him. But no tears. Just bright red anger and a lingering remorse that something could have been done if eager cooperation had existed. My carefully constructed machine was ruined.

I never saw Lieut. Tony Ceresa again. I was informed he was sent back to Regiment for reassignment. That was probably the best for all concerned. I could never have served with him again, and it didn't matter who was at fault that September day. Some of us were still alive. We had to keep going.

Most of what happened that day is now blocked out. It's true, we remember mostly pleasant things and tend to discard most of the ugly. Especially repugnant to me, in retrospect, was killing by shooting in the back. To me, snipers have always been the scumbags of war--and yet I realize they can be useful in certain defensive situations, particularly where the enemy has penetrated. That's how we got caught .

The German Army praised and rewarded its snipers. In a captured document in Normandy,[1] the commander of Hitler's 8th Parachute Regiment said:

"Exact accounts are to be kept by our sharpshooters. At 25 certified kills the sharpshooter concerned is to be recommended for decoration with the Iron Cross Second Class. If the sharpshooter does not reach that number of kills, then a day's special furlough should

[1] *29 Let's Go, Ibid*

be granted for each two certified kills in addition to his regular furlough."

This attitude and treatment of "sharpshooters," really snipers, was probably much more realistic than mine. Like me, most Americans in our civilian armed forces were probably were guilty of playing at war. Not the Germans.

But some few Americans like General Patton loved the heat of battle. He once said:

"To be bombed, strafed, machine-gunned or shelled was exhilarating. Compared to war, all other forms of human endeavor shrink to insignificance."

Even the debris of war excited Patton.[2] Coming out of Avranches with his aide, Lt. Col. Charles Codman, Patton passed burned fields, a series of twisted trucks and tanks, half-tracks and ambulances reeking with rotting German bodies, ruined farms and devastated buildings with bloated carcasses of farm animals and cows laying everywhere. He turned to Codman and said, "Could anything be more magnificent?"

It is true that there's no emotion or "lift/high" that can compare with leading troops in battle. Over the years I've tried most of them and the feelings have never remotely approached those reached in World War II crisis situations. Maybe that's the counterpoint to the dangers of combat command. In those days we had little time to philosophize.

Medals were another thing America's infantry fighting men never thought too much about until confronted with headquarters' need for awarding them. Every so often G Company--and all other rifle companies, I presume--would receive directives from Regiment or Division saying that we were falling behind in citations. Nothing more need be said. Battalion and company commanders knew the remedies and sometimes passed the word down to the platoon sergeants and lieutenants. Otherwise they anointed their staffs.

One such hint came to me following our disastrous

[1,2] *29 Let's Go! Ibid*
2 Delivered from Evil, Ibid

loss day. The platoon was down to less than 20 men this time, not all of them well; the company had less than 100 actives and our collective noses had just been bloodied. We sat looking at La Trinite and Fort Montbarey just above it and wondered if it all was worth the effort. Ordinarily, we would have ignored the medals hint, but we did have a day or two of holding our positions with not much to do but seethe, so why not?

I would have given Olencki a medal if I could figure he did more than do his job superbly and offer inspiration to everyone else. Headquarters doesn't award medals for that, unfortunately.

Sergeant Perkins did take on more responsibility than he normally did, and under sniper fire he helped get our automatic rifle team into position. He was a rock when we needed one. So I put him in for a Silver Star. I believe he finally got a Bronze Star, one step down in valor rankings. The whole platoon should have received these.

I remember agonizing about whether or not I should write a letter to Olencki's folks. What I was going to say to Olencki's father, Walt?

Same first name as his son; they must have been close. Then there was a sister. Olencki had promised to set me up with her when we returned . What do I say to her? That her brother was shot in the back because I went too far too fast?

I just couldn't tell the Olenckis that their guy was shot in the back by a sniper. It didn't sound right as an ending moment for a great kid. So I finally wrote that Walt, Jr., had died in an attack on a fortified enemy position, that he was an inspiration to all the men and that he served with distinction. I said he was a credit to his family and I would look up Walter, Sr., when I got back and tell him more.

I don't know if he ever got the letter. I left it with the Company for mailing and I was out of action myself within two days.

When I got back to New York a year and a half later, I looked for a Walter Olencki in the Manhattan and Brooklyn phone books. I never found a listing. Sadly, I dropped the Olenckis and I've regretted not doing more to find them since.

That night I finished the hole Olencki had started for us. Part of the ground was still wet from his blood, and I carefully placed it to one side. I remember looking at the small pile and realizing that was all we had left of a good friend. I bent down and actually kissed that pile of blood and mud that dark night. There were some silent tears, too.

On September 3 and 4, a Sunday and Monday, we sat in our holes and waited. Meantime, we were catching heavy mortar and artillery fire--and there was a pesky machine gun set up on the other side of La Trinite which cut loose every time somebody in our lines moved. It was too long range to be much more than a nuisance, which it certainly was.

There was no German counterattack. It made us think that maybe we had Jerry on his heels. Certainly there was no action in La Trinite during the daylight hours, and for good reason. We were close enough to pop anybody moving in the town. So were the Krauts.

Both sides patrolled vigorously after dark, but actually avoided contact. Like two dogs circling, looking for a sign of weakness in the other. I figured we could take La Trinite easily and deny Jerry a listening post. But where do we go from there? We all knew that every footprint beyond the village would be uphill and blood-stained.

By mid-day on the 4th, our move had been decided. A night attack, beginning that midnight, with the limited objectives of La Trinite and the high ground behind it. How far? Until you're stopped, I was told by Herrick.

My Third Platoon would lead one column of two platoons on the left flank, next to the highway. Another column of platoons, including the First Platoon, weapons and headquarters people, would be on the right under the command of Lieutenant Herrick.

We were to contact Herrick's group on the other side of La Trinite and continue the uphill attack. Fox Company, again on our left, was to guide on us and be responsible for those buildings on the left side of the highway. And, I voiced at the Battalion meeting, for keeping up with us.

Americans were accustomed to fighting at night--not so for the Germans. We felt we had the advantage in night attacks, particularly true in this situation. We were going into a heavily-fortified hedgerow defense area, with every defense point automatically zeroed-in by Kraut heavy weapons and artillery. If we had mounted the same attack in daylight, we would need tremendous artillery support, possibly even the fighter-bombers. Casualties would be heavy, that was sure.

Our battalion command thought we could sneak to large ground gains with a night attack before the Germans were really aware that this was more than a routine patrol action.

It might work--if we didn't show our firepower. So we agreed that we would not fire our guns except in emergency. Our main weapon would be the grenade. We each drew several, along with a white cloth to wrap around our left arms above the elbow for night identification purposes.

Everyone nixed a broad front night attack. Such a wide formation was nearly impossible to control. True, the narrow attack columns might miss some dug-in Germans along the way. It was agreed that the lead columns would not stop. Follow-up units would neutralize any enemy the attack columns missed.

We dropped off all loose and possibly rattling equipment and some of us even blackened our faces early. We could have saved the effort. The night turned out dark, with no moon.

George Company shoved off shortly after midnight. Sergeant Edwards was the first, or point man in our column. I was second; then came two platoon reliables as our backup. Sergeant Perkins was fifth in line. He headed the rest of the two platoons and would not advance until we front people secured the next hedgerow or objective. This sequence went house by house in La Trinite, which we cleared in less than 15 minutes. Not a German in sight. No hints of opposition. No mines or booby-traps. It was too quiet.

We heard F Company on our left. They were doing well. No action there either. The highway was deserted. I looked to the right. It was a black nothing. No sign of

Herrick. I stopped the column and passed the word for
Perkins to come up. I asked him to send a couple of men
over to contact Herrick and to take a defensive position at
the far edge of town. We would wait for our right flank
this time.

The night was quiet. There was no artillery from
either side. Off in the distance there was a rumble or two,
but nothing in our area. All of a sudden, from our
immediate right, came the rip sound of a German
Schmeisser. The Schmeisser shot so fast it sounded like
cloth tearing. That machine pistol sound always set me on
edge. I knew if anybody ever got caught in its spray, he
could have five bullets stitched in his body before he could
say "Schmeisser."

We froze. But nothing else happened. Quiet fell like
a smothering blanket. I wondered if our two scouts were
down--or if someone had spotted Herrick's group. There
was nothing we could do but wait, at the ready.

My favorite American weapon by this time was the
Thompson submachine gun, an adequate short-range
spray gun. It was the poor man's answer to the Schmeisser
and it dated back to the Capone days. With a cyclic rate of
fire about half that of the German weapon, it nevertheless
threw a heavy .45-caliber slug and, I thought, was much
better than the semi-automatic carbine which was World
War II officer issue. Most times I carried a Tommy and a
.45 Colt automatic pistol. I had to leave the Tommy behind
that night, and I missed the security feeling it gave me.

Maybe five minutes had passed since the
Schmeisser, and one of our contact men to Herrick
returned. Herrick wanted to keep the other messenger in
case he had to find us again. The returning man told us
the Schmeisser was nothing--a nervous German
outposting, apparently alone, who was quickly taken
captive when Herrick's column stumbled into him
accidentally. No one was hurt, our man said. The Heinis
probably didn't know yet about our attack.

From the last building in La Trinite, Edwards and I
did a lot of looking and some scouting before we decided
to advance our column tight along the right side of the
highway. It seemed to become a sunken road the closer it
got to Fort Montbarey. If we drew a fight, I reasoned, it

would come along the road. Better that than leaving an enemy strongpoint behind us. Edwards and I agreed that when and if we had opposition we would sideslip one field to the right and continue our penetration, sealing the strongpoint with a squad if we could. We moved out; same formation.

Edwards was three or four strides in front of me and I could barely see his white armband. Behind me were a couple of scouts, then Sergeant Perkins and the two platoons, maybe a total of 50 to 60 men. all of us moving as quietly as we could.

Our advance group was to clear the field and the hedgerow immediately in front before the following platoons would move forward. Edwards and I decided we would go over hedgerows together, with our two scouts standing support a few yards away.

The first hedgerow and field went fairly easy. We made too much noise going over that mini-mountain, I figured, but it couldn't be avoided, climbing and then sliding down tangled, heavy growth on both sides of a 10-foot mound in the middle of a dark night. Jerry could certainly hear us coming unless everyone over there was asleep.

The second hedgerow mound was now in front of us. Edwards and I began climbing together and we made it with muttered curses. A good thing we didn't have our rifles or carbines to carry. Our two support guys had theirs strapped to their bodies, but Edwards and I had nothing but grenades and our pistols. We made it without a lot of noise and as soon as our two trailing men got over, we messaged to the rear, Then all of us started in a ragged formation across the field to the next hedgerow.

We had managed a little over half of the field when the Germans opened up on us. I saw the machine gun muzzle flashes as I hit the ground. They came from the corner of the field next to the road. If the Krauts had waited another 10 seconds they would have had us all at point blank range. As it was I heard a heavy threshing from the soldier behind me. I sneaked a look around as sporadic firing from the machine gun continued. Everyone was prone that I could see. There wasn't much we could do. The gun was out of grenade throwing range and we were caught in the middle of a barren field.

"Lieutenant, you okay?" That was Edwards.

"Yeah," I answered.

"I'm hit and I got to get out of here," he continued.

"Bad?" I asked.

"Don't think so but I'm bleeding. Cover me. I'm going back."

I fired several rounds from my pistol at the machine gun position, then rolled over three or four times so they couldn't get a muzzle-flash fix on me.

Edwards rushed by, weaving and remembering to run as low to the ground as possible. I ground-squirmed back to the soldier behind me. He was lying motionless. No sign of life there. I lifted his head--his face and throat was a pulpy, wet mess.

We had to get out of this situation. We couldn't fight from our position, and neither could the platoon give us any help without disclosing a lot of firepower.

I wheeled on my knees and, pushing off, starting running back to Perkins' hedgerow.

"Go back. Get back'" I shouted as I ran, zigging and zagging, back to that hedgerow we had just left. Our remaining scout made it just as fast as I did, if not faster.

The Jerry machine gun was firing at us all this time but the black night helped us. It must have been very difficult for the Krauts to see anything more than a dozen yards away. They were spraying the landscape.

Perkins and I spread the men behind our hedgerow. I was thinking counterattack, even at night. But nothing happened. Even the German machine gun quieted. I'm guessing that they thought they had an enemy patrol in their sights and "we certainly sent them scrambling" or whatever words Krauts used to declare a complete victory.

The story I heard later that night--or even a couple of months down the road when I returned to the Company, I can't remember exactly when I heard it--was that the German machine gun crew who opened up on us came in for surrender, waving their white scarves, later that night after we by-passed them with the main attack. They were Russians, they said, forced to fight the "Amis." They purposefully shot over our heads and before we got too close, claiming that if they wanted to they could have killed all of us. They figured this plea would help, even save their lives (most German troops were told that if they were captured they would be put to death by the Americans--and many believed it).

I hope their story worked, because I am inclined to believe it was at least partially true, especially the more I think about it. They did hit Sergeant Edwards and kill the man behind me but I believe that they then misdirected their fire. There's no question they were not really effective when they could have been and that they were spraying the landscape when they had us pinned down, defenseless.

Perk and I decided to continue our attack, but one hedgerow in from the highway. I was going ahead, as the point, Perkins would follow me with a couple of men. Our rule held: No weapons would be fired, except in emergency.

We were about ready to move out when we heard movement to our right. We crouched, at the ready, with all weapons pointing toward the sounds. Then somebody saw white armbands. It was Herrick's platoon. There were some welcome words. I quieted everyone as best I could, and asked where Lieutenant Herrick was.

Just a couple of minutes later I found him in an unoccupied cow shed (the bovine residents were probably at Fort Montbarey, live or in steak form). Cowboy was standing ankle deep in cow turds, and I remember I had a few choice words for his choice of a command post.

Herrick thought we ought to combine forces to increase our firepower potential, now that Jerry probably knew he was facing strong patrol action or even worse for him, a night attack. I agreed, believing that if we could establish a strong defensive position a few hedgerows up the hill, we could create havoc with German actions the following day. Imagine, waking up to discover an enemy company was behind your lines. And we had an artillery forward observer officer with us. He could give our Battalion howitzers and Division heavy stuff one of their best days with just a few radioed map coordinates on Heini troop concentrations or gun positions.

I figured Herrick and I would lead this new advance and I asked him if he wanted my Third Platoon to back us.

He replied: "You bring your group over here. Leave a squad to watch the machine gun and let us know if they move or if there's anything doing on the road. Let's get started up the hill, one hedgerow in from the road, your platoon first.; Second Platoon follows you and watches our right side. First Platoon back. Pass the word. Quick."

Within a few minutes we were ready and the Cowboy moved out, alone. I was right behind, and my platoon followed us by a few yards. We were now closed up, compared to our earlier formations, and it did bring more firepower to bear on the attack point. I felt less alone.

This closeness didn't last long, however. The Cowboy began disappearing in the dark ahead of me.

5

England? Hello Again

*If the German bullet had not been intercepted
by my pointed pistol, it would have
hit me square in the face*

I can still see George Herrick with those long
Ichabod scarecrow legs and flapping arms heading into the
night. His Company followed, like dutiful schoolboys out
for a disciplinary hike.

We were well inside German lines by this time, but
there was no hesitation. Herrick was so tall and gangly
that he could scale many of the hedgerows easily--or more
easily than those of us who had to use considerable
physical strength to pull ourselves up and over. He could
cover a lot of ground with those long legs, too.

Herrick must have been almost a hedgerow field
ahead of me before I realized it. I couldn't see him or his
white arm band.

There was nothing to do but bring the Company
along in the same direction, uphill and into Jerry's craw. I
thought we would run into our missing leader before long.
Sure enough, squatting in the corner of the next hedgerow
was the Cowboy.

"I heard something moving on the other side," he
pointed up and whispered in my ear. "We'd better go slow

from here."

"Do you want me to bring 'em up for an attack?" I figured we were now well beyond the forbidden use of our weapons, especially if we were running into major enemy forces.

"No. Let's you and me go over quietly right here. Bring up some people to back us."

I passed the word back to Perkins to send up an automatic weapons team with another three to four riflemen. It took a little while before I heard movement behind us. In the meantime I was eyeing the hedgerow in front of us. It was larger than most I had seen, maybe twice my height. But the sides seemed to slope more than the average hedgerow, too. Crawling, we could make it.

I had a grenade in my left hand, pin not pulled. In my right was my pistol, ready to fire. Herrick was maybe two or three paces to my left and ready to start the climb. I pointed up with my gun hand. He nodded and we began crawling. It was tougher than I had expected. The grenade was in my pocket by this time, and I was just getting ready to snap on the pistol's safety and put it in my other jacket pocket in order to use my right hand for more upward pulling power. . . Then it happened.

There was a large explosion just above me and to my left front. I looked up immediately to see Herrick's body tumbling backwards. I could see a black shape on top of the hedgerow, just a few feet away. I raised and swung the Colt and I pulled the trigger, twice. There was an immediate hot blast on my gun hand, like somebody had hit it with a red-hot tire iron. I thought my pistol had blown up. Then, as I slid to the base of hedgerow, I looked again for my target. There was no shape, no more shots. I heard some seemingly far-away shouts and the muffled thunder of running steps on the other side of the hedgerow.

Several of our grenades sailed over my head to land on the other side of the hedgerow; I remember hearing the fuse pops, but I don't remember hearing the explosions. By this time I had my grenade in my left hand, and gave it a toss over the big hedgerow. I don't remember whether or not I pulled the pin--and if I did, how. My right hand was a wet, bloody mess. I could see a protruding thumb, that's about all.

Cradling my right arm, I scooted on my left side over to where the Cowboy lay. He was unconscious and looked to be seriously hurt with a bullet to his chest, point blank range. A couple of men were already with him and were figuring on how to get him out of there. I was thinking the same thing, and told one of them to get to Perkins to tell him to get the men back to the last hedgerow we had crossed and set up a three-sided perimeter defense. Whether we liked the terrain or not, this was where we were stopping for rest of the night.

My hand was numb, the pain somewhat gone, but not the bleeding. Two of our company men poured sulfa powder over it, gave me a batch of sulfa pills to wash down with my stale, tepid canteen water. They brought out some white gauze bandages and started wrapping. The hand rapidly became a huge hunk of bandage.

Several of my guys were enthusiastic as we retreated to our safety hedgerow. "You got him, Lieutenant," they said excitedly. "He got Lieutenant Herrick, but you got him."

By this time I had discarded, correctly as it turned out, the theory that my pistol had exploded. The Heini's bullet must have hit my pistol and shattered into my hand (it was German lead the doctors took out of the hand later). If that bullet had not been intercepted by my hand holding that pistol, it would have hit me square in the face. But I wasn't thinking about possibilities that early September morning, but primarily about getting the Company organized for defense and then about getting myself back to an aid station.

It was good to believe that I had taken out the German who got Herrick, but I'll never know. I do know it would be difficult not to hit him; he was just seven to eight feet away. We must have fired at each other at the same time or within milli-seconds. His bullet shattered into the right side of my pistol. That meant I may have fired to his right on both of my shots, especially the second, swinging left too far. And I may have missed him completely. I didn't dwell on it, only in hindsight and in evaluation of angles as I later replayed the action.

I recall finding Perkins in that confused black night.

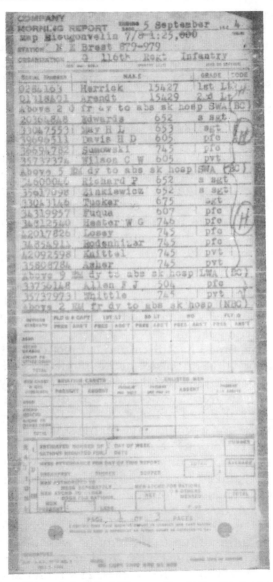

Herrick and I headed a list of 22 casualties in the September 5, 1944 morning report for Company G, 116th Infantry. SWA stands for seriously wounded in action; LWA for lightly wounded. Company strength was less than 120 total (starting with nearly 180 less than a week earlier). The following morning's counterattack accounted for most of the casualties listed here.

--Courtesy NationalPersonnel Records Center

"I think we've hit something big," I hoarsely warned him, and then described as best I could the running and muffled shouts from the German side of the hedgerow. He sent a runner back to find Lieutenant Bookless. Book was the guy in charge now.

Perkins told me Sergeant Edwards was okay. He was shot in the shoulder earlier, when we ran into the machine gun. Edwards was lucky--three or four wounds during his total European service and none really serious.

I was concerned about my hand, even to the point of wondering what it would be like to be without a right arm. I couldn't feel anything from my right elbow down.

The aid people didn't help my disposition. They kept tugging on my good arm to get me back to the aid station. Actually they needn't have been so persistent. I wanted to get the hell out of there as much as they did. I thought I was functioning fine, but I probably was on an adrenaline high. I knew I was losing a lot of blood. The heavy gauze bandage was mostly black with soaked-through blood by now.

Bookless came up shortly and I think we talked about the situation. He had a tech sergeant, Wilson Carr, with him. And he had a company of less than 100 men stuck out like a sore thumb, again, from the main body. At least one of his flanks was open, maybe two. Our route to the rear was secure, I was told.

And then, suddenly, I became a casualty--weak, unable to think or speak much, wandering mentally and physically, shaking. The battle crisis high was gone. I was glad to leave.

An aid man helped me walk back to the Battalion aid station. It was stumbling progress down the Brest-Le Conquet highway, back through La Trinite. The blacktop was deserted. A walk in blackness, but at least in the right direction, I thought. And I also remember, I was actually concerned about mines on that road as we moved along it.

It must have been close to three in the morning when we arrived at the aid station, only a couple hundred yards behind La Trinite. The aid man, whose name I knew then but have forgotten by now, supported me when I staggered or stumbled, but we made it, again as I recall, without much trouble.

"Don't let them take the hand, Doc" I said to Captain Herter as he unwrapped the dark red mess of a bandage. A small-framed man, Captain Herter was Puerto Rican. I had met him before, but only briefly. He gave me a needle, probably morphine, while he asked how it happened. I gave him a short account. Then he replied in his staccato Spanish-accented speech:

"Somebody's going to have to do some work on this, but you'll be all right."

"Save it--can they save it?" I asked.

"You must have a lot of lead in there," he replied, pointing to a gigantic swelling in the fleshy part of the hand between the thumb and index finger. "Can you move your fingers?"

I could, just a fraction of an inch, maybe more of a twitch, and I did it.

"You'll be okay."

That's as much as I could get from Herter. He rebandaged the hand and said an ambulance would be picking me up in a few minutes for a ride back to an evacuation hospital. Then he left.

There were a few wisps of light gray in the east when I finally boarded the ambulance. I must have dozed off a bit in the aid station. Another two or three wounded were in the gut wagon, waiting. I didn't know them. We took off on a jerky, bumpy ride--it seemed like cross country. My only answer was to close my eyes and pretend I was someplace else, and it must have worked. When the ambulance finally stopped to unload it was broad daylight outside and I didn't remember much of what must have been a brutal ride for everyone else.

We were at an Army field hospital, probably near a smaller town in the Brest area. There were no road signs and I really didn't care where we were anyway. My bandage was blood-soaked again. This time it looked horrible to me. I began to worry about the amount of blood I was losing. The hand didn't really pain as much as my psyche, which was already blackly visualizing how I would manage the rest of my life as a left-hander.

When we got out of the ambulance we were herded to an area to wait, for what I don't know, but I presumed it was to see a doctor. Most of us there were walking wounded and we had a low priority, even though a red tag on the front of my uniform carried the large letters SWA, or Seriously Wounded in Action.

The tag, I found, was an automatic passport to most any activity in the hospital area. I wandered about freely, my arm in a tight sling to hold it almost in front of my face. No longer was it really hurting.

I found a chapel and spent some time there asking the Lord to save my hand and arm. Mostly I was at peace alone in the chapel. Humbled a bit, too. And I didn't forget to thank Him for saving my life. Several times I did that. And I prayed for Olencki and others in George Company. I began feeling better.

A chow line was my next pleasant discovery. I hadn't had any real food for two days. In front of me was a spread of scrambled eggs, bacon and pancakes, with what looked like maple syrup. Coffee, toast and marmalade, too. Another G. I. helped me overfill a plate, with a lot of everything. I sat down to eat, for the first time using my left hand.

A few mouthfuls were enough. I was shoveling it in when I became gut-wrenching sick so fast I couldn't move a muscle before I vomited into the ground beside me and the plate propped in front of me A hospital man hurried over and helped me clean up and cover the mess. He was blaming himself not seeing me take the full plate.

"I should have stopped you," he said. "The stomach gets used to K-rations and not eating much or regularly, and a sudden feast really upsets it. Take it easy with the food for a few days, then you can eat all you want."

Surprisingly, after I had upchucked I wanted another go at the same food line. Better sense prevailed-- besides a medical assistant for the hospital right then began taking my medical history. He said the field hospital surgeons would remove all the metal in my hand they could, but it likely would be impossible to get it all if, as they thought, the Heini bullet pulverized into my hand.

He said he had looked at the X-rays with the surgeon and the doctors believed the hand could be saved, without a doubt. What functions I would have with it later were impossible to say now but he predicted a near-full recovery. He added that if the doctors here thought they were not qualified to handle a delicate hand operation, they would send me back to an Army General Hospital in England or even back to the States.

I liked what I heard, particularly the part about going back home. Shortly after he gave me a pre-op shot I was feeling very good, even to joking with the surgical team before their sodium pentothal injection moved in to lay down a blanket of unconsciousness.

When I woke I was lying on my back in a cot near the side of a large tent. I remember that the tent sides were rolled up and a brilliant sun was bouncing its light everywhere. It was warm and comfortable. My hand was still there, on top of my O.D. blanket in plain view and bandaged heavily. I didn't hurt in any way; I dozed off.

Several times in the next few hours I awakened, only to fall off again. I knew I was in a moving vehicle and I knew I was going somewhere, where I didn't care. At one stop, I turned my head to look out of a window and I saw what appeared to me to be a New England fishing port. Nets and buoys on docks, boats with sails and fishnet outriggers and always, the screaming, wheeling gulls. By this time I had raised myself and started looking for anything familiar. Soon I spotted the word "Morlaix" on a sign. Morlaix was a Brittany port on the north coast, about 30 to 40 miles from Brest. So I was going to get an evacuation ride to Britain by boat.

The ambulance moved on, however, and we finally stopped a few minutes later in what seemed to me the middle of an empty field. There was a muffled roar of big engines ahead. The word came back that our ambulance was backed up to a C-47 twin-engine cargo plane evidently converted to a hospital carrier.

Those of us who could walk left our ground transportation and mounted a ramp to the plane. I remember we were given our choice of walking or being stretcher-borne to the plane; I chose walking.

There were stacked bunks along each side of the interior and a table with chairs at the rear. The walking wounded sat at the table and the loading of stretchers took less than 10 minutes. Nurses appeared from nowhere and took charge. Aside from the too-busy nurses at the field hospital these were the first American women I had seen in a month. It was pleasant experience just to watch them and feel their smiles. Before takeoff a couple of them came back to sit with us. Sharp looking, they must have gone to some trouble to keep themselves neat and attractive for us chewed-up guys. They told us we were headed for an Army general hospital in the British Midlands, not far from Birmingham, my old stomping grounds.

Evidently the Army field hospital had passed on trying to remove lead from my hand and deferred the operation to the larger general hospital. That was okay with me. I knew it would be a delicate procedure, one that required some experience in hand surgery. The operation, I was informed, was scheduled for tomorrow.

My arrival and move to the hospital ward is somewhat lost in my memory. I do remember another sodium pentothal injection on the hospital operating table the next day. And I remember waking up under clean sheets, feeling no pain and, generally, a lot more conscious of what was happening.

The huge lump of steel in the soft flesh between my thumb and forefinger was gone. In its place was a deep cut, left open for saline washings which were to occur several times every day--and night. I had trouble moving my fingers, some of which had deep cuts. In brief, the hand looked horrible. I couldn't examine it closely.

Therapy began almost immediately, however, and the string of constant and painful exercises for 60 to 90 minutes daily seemed to help, gradually.

The doctors said I still had lots of lead in the hand. They didn't go after some fragments for fear of cutting nerves. An X-ray of the hand showed what must have been hundreds of these tiny particles, some almost like dust, still scattered throughout the hand and even into the wrist.

My folks hadn't heard from me in nearly a month, I realized. By this time they may have received the War Department telegram announcing their son had been seriously wounded in action--and they must be going through worries multiplied by worries.

Obviously I couldn't write with my right hand. So I'll do it left-handed, I decided. And I'll print so they can read it.

After I finished I reviewed the left-handed effort and it was messy and bad. I could imagine what my mother would think, regardless of what I said, when she got that letter. The upshot of all this was that I dictated to my nurse my first letter home. Together we did several more and it got to be fun, at least for me.

I remember I had a special feeling for that ward nurse. She was petite, with big, dark-brown eyes. She handled most of my therapy and saline solution applications, too. At one time I thought I was in love, but I probably would have fallen in love at that time with any attractive female who smiled at me more than once. I remember making a mild approach to her at one time and getting a professional nursing response, which is as it should be.

We did go to the hospital's officers club several times together and had great times, but it always was a relationship between a care-giver and a patient. I found other fields in which to play and she--well, I think she was smart enough to know that most of her patients developed a crush on her.

Hospital life is never dull unless the patient stays too long. That would not be the case here. From the beginning, everyone on the hospital staff talked about how soon we could be back with our units. With good reason, I suppose, they bragged about how fast their "turn-around" time was.

There was plenty of effort by these hospital eager beavers. Every four hours, regardless of what I was doing, I got a penicillin shot. Every morning, for more than an hour, I did painful physical therapy exercises with my hand. The staff even had walking patients out for morning constitutionals and was pushing for calisthenics. I saw the point of all of this but balked at the exercises. Eventually I was shamed into doing the whole bit.

Fellow patients really make the difference in hospital stays, too. My ward mates came from a world of backgrounds. One was a fortiesh captain who was just getting ready for action with a late-arriving infantry unit when he suffered a severe appendicitis attack. He had the appendix cut out and he was probably the sickest man in a ward filled with battle-wounded.

Another patient was a young lieutenant, about my age, who was shot through his right lung. He spent every night on a fluid removal machine. Horrible sucking sounds, as I remember. I hoped Cowboy Herrick wasn't going through this, if he was still alive.

A third wardmate was a Free French sous-lieutenant or warrant officer, I never knew which. He had serious leg wounds and would probably never walk again without crutches. He needed an artificial limb, but the French Army didn't seem to believe it, so he continued to lurch around on his crutches and one semi-functioning leg.

He really lived to get back to his tank. He was hit just before General Leclerc's Free French were to stage their triumphal march through Paris. He had a wife and family there whom he hadn't seen in more than five years, he said. Jean was his first name. I can't remember his surname.

Jean had been in uniform most of his life. He was at least 20 years older than I. He was a tank driver who had served in North Africa and who fought his way upward from the ranks. He didn't deny he had served in the Foreign Legion early in his military career.

My French got a bit of polishing from Jean. He did not speak English other than a few words, so I became his interpreter for anything more complicated than a drink of water.

I remember he didn't like DeGaulle whom he called *un Generale de Politique*; he hated *les Boches* and loved his *char*, or tank. He worried whether or not he was going to get a new one with all the equipment he had before. If he had been in the U. S. Army he needn't have worried; he was in no shape, or ever would be, to return to combat duty. I guessed the French would find a way to use an old soldier like Jean, even if it meant propping him up in a tank turret to direct fire.

Jean taught me that the French were not so much pro-English or pro-anything else as they were anti-

German. He was also bitter about the French people who worked for the Nazis during the occupation.

"Do you know," I remember his saying one day, "*Savais-vous qu' il y a des millions, oui, millions, des francaais quit sont travailler pour les allemands?*"

I knew or had heard that there were many Frenchmen who became rich or influential during the German occupation. These were black marketers, mainly, but they also included farmers, informers and the police (for example, there were 20 times as many French as German members of the uniformed German police force in France during the occupation.) The war also brought out the *baroudeurs*--literally, the brawlers, vicious soldiers of fortune who were only happy with guns, blood and loot.

Retribution came swiftly after the liberation. Denunciation, jailings and executions without trial went wild. Neighbors denounced neighbors, lovers' quarrels became life and death accusations and old-time political scores were settled simply by pointing fingers. It was easy to get rid of someone not liked by telling the patriots he or she was a *collaborateur*, no proof required. It was estimated that 30 to 40 thousand French people died in this way during the first few months after liberation. There can never be an accurate count.

Jean and I went into London together one weekend. It was a two-hour train ride from Salisbury, where we both visited the cathedral. I took Jean to the Red Cross club and then promptly lost him until I saw him back in the hospital the following Monday.

He never did say what he did during those three nights and two days, but I had my ideas. There was an aura of unleashed strength, violence and blood about the *beau et gentil* Jean and that, I knew, was attractive to many ladies. I'm sure he wasn't lonely in London.

Bandages were never placed on my hand and the sight of it, early on, was not encouraging. It was swollen, red, purple and black, with a three-inch gash from the index finger knuckle to the first thumb knuckle near my wrist. The cut seemed to go clear through to the palm. The doctors were pleased with my progress, however. They explained that I was involved in a relatively new medical procedure for hands which called for no stitching of wounds because of possible lesions. The saline solution, almost a constant soak, also seemed to be working.

They predicted a return to full duty in record time. I was not so sure. Without stitches my cut was slow in closing and that, in my opinion, delayed my return by a week or more. As it was, the wound was not closed when I started back to Germany in late November, about two and a half months after I began my hospitalization.

So I became one more plate in the medical fast-food line. I didn't protest too much, even though I was getting used to the easy hospital routine of checking medical needs every morning and then, later in my term there, disappearing for the rest of the day--and sometimes night.

Strangely, I even wanted to get back to the Blue and Gray, but it was to something I hoped would be better than hedgerow fighting. Attacking in Germany was different, but better? No way, I found out later.

In the meantime, life in the hospital rolled on.

6

Back Into Action

---

*George Company was so exhausted by morning
that we just walked away from the objective;
the Germans left, too. End of battle.*

---

*T*he highlight of my hospital stay in England was the mid-September arrival of the wounded of Operation Market Garden, an Allied airborne drop into Holland which basically failed.

This was a daring flanking move through the German defenses of the lower Rhine and which, if successful, would have shortened the war by months, if not have ended it when Allied troops reached German soil.

Defending this northern flatlands approach to Germany were troops relatively unscathed by the Normandy fighting. They retreated through Belgium and into refurbished defensive positions near the big bridges of the braided lower Rhine, at Eindhoven, Nijmegen and Arnheim. The Allied drop, using the 82nd and the 101st Airborne Divisions of the U. S. and the First British Airborne, was a well-planned surprise jump across 60 miles of wet flatlands leading up to the bridges. It anticipated a British rescue drive through the defending Germans to rescue the parachute divisions. That worked for Eindhoven and Nijmegen but, as the author Cornelius Ryan said, Arnheim was a bridge too far.

Our hospital was flooded with casualties from the 82nd Division, dropped at Nijmegen, the second bridge. Mostly, I believe, they were flown directly from the battle to the hospital.

I was at Intake when the first casualties arrived, primarily because Intake generally had some things going on dull Sunday mornings. This Sunday was not only active but overwhelming. I turned into a volunteer helper as did every semi-able bodied person in the hospital. Stretchers piled up in the hallways; still the flow kept coming.

My job was to classify the wounded roughly into "serious" and otherwise. Some of the walking wounded also pitched in to help us. By noon, the entire hospital was on alert with all personnel functioning. I thought they did a magnificent job.

Most newly-wounded men are hyper. I talked to them at length and tried to calm them. They could see I had been wounded, too, and that seemed to help. But they were young and angry because they felt they had let their buddies down by getting evacuated. The 82nd, I'll say, had great unit pride that day. All the men I saw were anxious to get back for another shot at Jerry. I would have been proud to have been a paratrooper in an outfit like the 82nd that day.

A few days after most of them had been transferred to other hospitals, I started an "estimate of the situation" thought process. This was the airborne's first operation since D-Day. Sure, they were always dropped into dangerous situations and their casualties were heavy, but generally they were out within a few days. And then they sat for weeks, even months, until the next big event.

In contrast, the average infantry division is in contact with the enemy until few are left, then it is propped up with replacements and stays on the line, fighting 24 hours a day. So it seems like an infantry G.I. is on fast forward forever. The only long-term relief is to be wounded--or die.

That's my future, too, I realized. So I began by believing that I could transfer to the paratroops. My inquiries were made to airborne people who always encourage anyone who wants to join their organization. I learned there was a jump school in England. Why not sign up? they asked. I was ready.

Everything was going well until I faced a senior

paratrooper officer. He said words to this effect:, "You are listed as an infantry unit leader and if you are any good at it and I think you are, then there's no way they'll release you. If you are not, then there's no way we'll take you. Better stay where you are. We couldn't accept your transfer request in any case."

After that I got set to return to the 116th--and, really, I felt good about the old outfit. By November, the hospital said I was ready to return. The 29th was in Germany by then; the Blue and Gray had linked with their old beach comrades, the First Infantry Division, to take Aachen and Wurselen, the first major German cities to fall to the Allies. By November, the Division had moved through most of the German coal and turnip field approaches to the Roer River.

I did manage to participate in a few social activities before my return, however. Visits to London were infrequent--too expensive and too many people. Instead I headed north to Birmingham, the Midlands city where I spent some time before crossing to Normandy the first time. There I found an old flame, a bus ticket taker who, she proudly announced to anyone who listened, was once a beauty queen. She had the English cream complexion, wide-set eyes and regular features. She also had what I called at the time, "large front bumpers." I could plainly see her attributes.

Actually I found her by remembering she hung out at a particular USO dance hall in downtown Birmingham. She had, since our earlier days and nights together, obviously cultivated her relations with other Americans. But when she saw me she allowed as how she "could spare a little time with an old chum."

We had a delightful weekend or two together. I rode on her bus (the top front left or right seat is not recommended on English double-decker buses if you scare easily by hanging in space 20 feet over crowded street corners) and visited her parents in their home. I learned that a Continental breakfast in wartime England consisted of ersatz juice, a near-unbreakable hard roll and a pot of tea. I did bring the family some marmalade, some real orange juice and a couple of cuts of meat from the hospital on one of my visits. Friendly and interesting, the family questioned me as much as I did them.

I found England in wartime warm and appreciative, most of the country as miniaturized as most of its people should be maximized. And it was forever green, as my home country in November is mostly brown, sometimes white.

There was one other factor: The 29th Division had been stationed in England since 1942 and the blue and gray patch I wore on my left shoulder was well-known and mostly admired. That just added to my good feelings about the Brits; they didn't forget.

The only negatives I found during my relatively brief stays with John Bull were the British press and news reels. If any stranger were to read and listen only to these public voices, he would reach the obvious conclusion that nothing was happening in the war unless the Brits were involved as heroes. I understand nationalism, but not so overwhelming--particularly when their partner, America, was by then carrying most of the manpower and materials burdens.

My journey back to George Company began in mid-November. The hospital literally pushed me out, with a large scale Band-Aid covering my open hand wound. I must say the hand was functioning properly and I was feeling no pain, but there it was, still raw flesh. So I bundled up, carried my right hand in a sling and accepted a long list of recommendations for its care. The doctors said it would take me two or three weeks to get back to my unit; by that time the wound would have closed.

I must say the wound did close within a week to 10 days after I rejoined George Company, a little over three weeks after I left the hospital. The hand, however, was still swollen and red.

For me, it was back through a "repple depple" and on board a ship. This time I sailed from Southampton on England's southern coast. Same pattern as last time, too. We crossed the channel in a large ship, then off-loaded into LCI's near the French coastline at LeHavre.

The City of LeHavre, once a major channel seaport,

lay in scattered, neat piles. I have never seen such wholesale destruction as I did in the city's port area. Even St. Lo had a few large piles; this city's waterfront was flat, but maybe this was because our engineer bulldozers had been in action.

We stepped over the few scattered bricks and small rubble piles and walked straight to a line of trucks. A few port troops were visible sweeping the dust, but otherwise there was nothing, even wrecked buildings, in sight. I never got to see the Heini final destruction of Brest, but I marveled at the thoroughness of the Germans in destroying LeHavre--or maybe it was the American bombing and aftermath cleanup. Even at that time, there were no wharves or docking facilities at LeHarve; we landed on a gravely, rough stone beach.

Our truck ride was short. We were deposited at a railhead a few miles into the countryside. Other truck convoys arrived, also carrying replacements and returning soldiers. We were loaded into boxcars--variations of the famous or infamous *quarante et huit* (40 men and/or eight mules) of World War I vintage. The resulting ride to Maastricht in eastern Holland took only a day and night to cover the necessary 250 miles, really quite fast for rail service in war-ravaged Europe.

I have conveniently forgotten about this exotic foreign rail travel segment. All I remember is lots of straw in the boxcars and a miserably cold trip that November in 1944.

My first questions at Division Rear involved what had happened after I left George Company in something of an isolated, exposed pickle in early September. The following morning, I learned, opened with a Jerry counter attack, preceded by heavy artillery and mortar fire. Our people were still down (probably asleep) in their hastily-prepared holes when a company-strength attack began just a hedgerow away. Sprinting toward our positions, the Germans likely would have wiped out George Company if it hadn't been for Tech Sergeant Wilson Carr. He was the first to spot the attack. He began firing and shouted for his platoon to get out of their holes and help.

Carr personally accounted for some dozen of the storming Germans; his platoon, belatedly, for more. And the Heinis never made it to our lines. They evaporated under murderous fire from a large part of George Company. Sergeant Carr received a Distinguished Service Cross for his work that day.

Fort Montbarey fell on September 16. It took flame-throwing tanks and truck loads of combat engineer explosives to penetrate that moated, multi-pillbox fort. After that happened the 116th found itself fighting house to house in Recouvrance, the Brest suburb near the submarine pens. Two days later Brest surrendered. Nothing resembling a port was left. General Ramcke and his combined forces had done their job in denying the Allies access to a major deep sea port in Western Europe.

Antwerp, Belgium, another port possibility, was taken on September 4, but it wasn't until late November that Canadian troops cleared Antwerp's Scheldt Estuary approaches so that deep draft vessels could unload their cargoes directly to land transport on the Continent. Thus Antwerp became the Allies' first major supply port. Our efforts for Brest were Army footnotes.

Brest, in effect, was a noble effort in a lost cause. Several days before our attack on the fortress city, General Bradley's planners concluded that the Brest garrison would probably fight to the end and leave nothing in the port city of any use to the Allies.

In truth, the farther east Patton's forces went, the less need for Brest's facilities. Patton realized this early on and would have left only a small force to isolate the city. Why, then, did we attack it? Not to take Brest would have meant a sizable German force in the Allied rear. Instead of calling off the Brest assault and pining General Ramcke with a smaller holding force, Bradley, for reasons he later admitted had more to do with prestige than military value, left VIII Corps behind to deal with the situation. Three of our top infantry divisions took on a larger German force in fortified positions, tough and well-supplied and disciplined. The American VIII Corps suffered nearly 10,000 casualties during the three-week all-out assault--and all for a key seaport which had committed

On September 12 and 13--a week after my exit from the battlefield--the 116th took Fort Montbarey, although it was another day or two before all 75 of the fort's occupants surrendered. Altogether, 138 500-pound bombs, plus four fire bombs, were dropped by fighter planes on this position. TNT and flame-throwing tanks were needed, too. Nothing much remained of Fort Montbarey except the moat.

-Photo from *29 Let's Go*

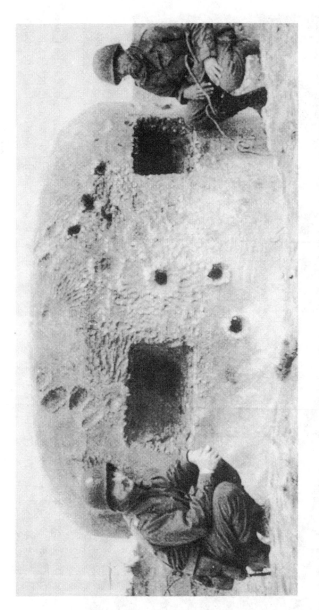

These 14-inch steel pill boxes protected the submarine pens at Brest. Direct hits by 57 mm and 75 mm guns could not penetrate the walls although they certainly shook up the Krauts inside.

---Photo from *29 PLet's Go*

Destruction of Brest's docks was so great that the Allies immediately gave up the idea of restoring it to a useful port city. Bottom is a view of the city's wrecked submarine pens from the landward side.

--29 Lets Go

suicide several weeks before.

General Bradley also became convinced, because of Brest, that the Germans would not give up easily. He wrote, "If she (Germany) could hold out so stubbornly for a lost cause such as Brest, what would happen when we reached her own borders or the Rhine River?"[2]

The Division was headed straight for that answer within a few days after the surrender of Brest.

And for me, a final salute to German General Hermann Ramcke. His defense of Brest was on a par with his defense of Monte Cassino in Italy. The conversion of sailors into good soldiers in a brief period was, in itself, a task well-done by the Germans. They fought well in a cause which must have been so obviously lost from its beginnings.

After the Brest campaign, the outfit had a few days rest, then boarded trains for the Siegfried Line in Germany, Aachen and the flat brown fields of northwest Germany leading up to the industrialized Rhine. Here the terrain was vastly different from the *bocage* or hedgerow country. Studded with village and farm clusters, the beet, cabbage and turnip fields stretched seemingly endlessly. Maastricht, a Dutch border town, was part of this world. We were well-treated in Maastricht, but we were cautious with the Dutch.

In a battlefield with a never-ending flat horizon, smart people control the high ground. I could see from Holland that this meant maximum use of church steeples and building roofs, anything taller than the muddy ground. Unfortunately, the Germans basically retained that control. And many of the villages and defense points, mostly less than a mile apart, were interconnected with chest-deep trenches. This was a network of strong points, protected by supply and retreat pathways. Again, the Americans faced difficult attack terrain.

We returnees were briefed on these problems as soon as we arrived in Maastricht. The Division's solution was to surround the village or strong point, cutting off all supply and retreat threats, then attack. It was the only tactical solution aside from leveling each village strong

---

[2] *Decision in Normandy*, by Carlo D'Este, E. P. Dutton

point from afar with our artillery. This we did, too. It was the easy solution, and most German villages east of the Roer River ended that winter as rubble piles. Needless to say, our troops rarely saw German civilians.

Our regiments were supposed to come and get us, but it was around Thanksgiving then and it was no-show, at least for those of us from the 116th, for a couple of days. It wasn't until December 1 that I got back to George Company.

The month of November had taken a lot out of the old outfit--for that matter, the entire Division. Rainfall in the Rhineland was twice normal for that month. One cold and wet, drizzly day seemed to spawn another. Mud was everywhere.

I read in company faces a degree of frustration I had never seen before. The Germans had put on a successful, manpower-consuming defense, once again, on the flatland farming country leading up to the Roer River.

Casualty numbers were climbing. George Company strength totaled 110 when I rejoined. Five days later it was down to 70. Company casualties weren't all from enemy action. Exposure, trench foot and sickness in the cold and wet inhospitable climate took its toll. In addition, the flow of fresh manpower, in the form of replacements, was ebbing.

Not so true for my old companions. Sergeants Edwards and Carr, both wounded at Brest, reported for action during the next few days, as did Sergeant Perkins, wounded at Aachen.

Major Charles Cawthon, our battalion commander at Brest, was out, seriously wounded by shellfire at Wurselen. Most everyone figured he would be back, but not soon. Cawthon had been with the regiment since it was federalized in 1941. Most of the Virginians carried an indefinable loyalty to the 29th. Oldtimers told this story about then-Captain Cawthon on D-Day:

The captain, at the time commanding a battalion headquarters company, took a shell fragment in his right facial cheek shortly after he landed. Later that day he took

One of a series of trenches dug by the Germans leading to and from nearly every Heini town. It was nearly impossible to shut down escape, except by surrounding the village and calling in artillery before attacking. Below is Battery C of the 110th Field Artillery, primary support for the 116th. On November 23, the Battery fired its 100,000 round of the war.

--Photos from *29 Let's Go*

another fragment in his left cheek, thus creating two holes in his face.

It was only natural that the story got around, and eventually got into the press, that a captain on Omaha Beach had been shot through the mouth when it was wide open--and not a tooth disturbed. Cawthon never had time to deny the story. So it stands today.

I learned that Lieutenant Herrick had returned to the outfit since I left, then had taken sick and had to be evacuated. The Kraut bullet that had felled him had passed entirely through his body without touching a vital organ-- and he had returned to full duty before me.   I   couldn't believe it--another medical miracle!

Lieutenant Jack Bookless was the only company officer that I recognized. Our new captain was a school teacher type named Orville Keyes. Captain Keyes went through the Aachen campaign, receiving two minor wounds and two Silver Stars for individual heroism. He was quiet and laid back. We got along well, as I recall, but because we were in a basic spread defense situation most of my second tour, I never really saw that much of him.

Division had reached the Roer River on November 28. Directly in our path, on its far bank on the high ground, was the ancient fort city of Julich, named after Julius Caesar. The Krauts still had several strong points on our side of the river, however. Reducing these became a major continuing task because the Germans would always re-establish them overnight, or even the next day. From their high ground positions, they controlled all daylight movements.

George Company was occupying the town of Koslar, near the west bank of the Roer and about 2,000 yards short of Julich, when I arrived. My platoon command post was an abandoned railroad station on slightly elevated ground north of Koslar. Someone had hollowed out a space below the ruined station's waiting room, now a pile of bricks. This nook became our CP (command post) and our gathering point for the entire platoon, holed out in the area surrounding the station throughout the cold nights. The wrecked station was a bit warmer and more comfortable.

We also took turns watching the Germans, as they undoubtedly did with us. This was nighttime living. We patrolled and moved only then. We slept most of the days. Our platoon position came under heavy but sporadic artillery fire during the days, probably because we were on the only comparatively high ground Jerry could see easily. If one of our men moved from foxhole to foxhole or to the CP we would get incoming. Most of us got used to it.

One man couldn't take it. A Virginian, he was one of my squad leaders--a staff sergeant if I remember rightly. Sgt. Elmer Rice had come in on Omaha Beach, been wounded and sent back and forth from hospitals at least a couple of times since then. An excellent soldier. He developed, over a period of time, a terrified reaction to big artillery. He would get out of his hole and run around the platoon area whenever artillery began falling. We finally had someone designated to sit on him when the shellings came. But it often didn't work. We couldn't catch him.

It was with the idea of not letting him hurt himself that I approached the battalion medical officer, still the Puerto Rican Captain Herter. He said the sergeant had worn out his resistance and recommended Rice be sent back for hospital observation. His was the few true cases of battlefield exhaustion that I ever saw, but I had heard about this condition being used as an excuse to escape combat duty. I don't think Sergeant Rice was faking; in fact, I know he wasn't. He had proved himself too many times before.

On December 6, a Wednesday, George Company was ordered to attack the Hassenfeld Gut, a cluster of two or three buildings on the west side of the river. This was one of those pesky Jerry strongpoints on our side of the river which the Germans kept reoccupying. It seems we had been battling forever over this trampled ground--or rather, this trampled oozing, semi-frozen mud. And again, it could only be a night attack. It would be suicide to try it in daylight under the Jerry guns.

The Germans let us get to within 100 yards before

In often futile attempts to limit German night time activities (minelaying, barbed wire stringing, etc.) on the pool-table flat lowlands leading to the Roer, the Division created "artificial moonlight" through the use of powerful searchlights. Mostly, the beams were banked against the heavy cloud cover. Sometimes it worked. At right, the Pier Station near Koslar served as my platoon headquarters much of this "stand-down" time. We considered it a luxury.
--*Photos 29 Let's Go*

This former coal mine building in Alsdorf, Germany, became the hot-shower headquarters for the Division. We trooped back here at least once a week, or, rather, hopefully once a week. Another activity we much appreciated was the dance routine back in Holland. We got back one time during those miserable weeks in Germany.

--Photos from *29 Let's Go*

they opened up with all of their pre-arranged fire patterns. We hit that cold slop face down and began firing back at the stone walls surrounding the Gut. Some of our guys dove into Heini minefields and had to be dragged out feet first. I remember thinking of World War I. So it's No Man's Land as we tried, unsuccessfully, to close in on walls spouting machine gun fire and heavens raining steel.

Here's how Lieutenant Reagor, CO of K Company, Third Battalion, described the scene 24 hours earlier, when that company tried to take the same Gut:[1]

"Before midnight the company was going southeast toward the Gut when the three-man company point unit ran into a minefield 150 yards from the buildings. As soon as the mines exploded German artillery came down in the area and a number of men were lost.

"It was so dark the men could not see the trip wires. If a man threw himself to the ground to avoid the artillery he was likely to fall on a mine. In the flash of exploding shells I saw men who remained standing in the artillery barrage, risking shell fragments in preference to the danger of tripping mines.

"At 3 A.M. on December 5 twenty men were sent through the minefield to attack from the north. There were more explosives in the minefield, more artillery fell, and later there was more machine gun and rifle fire. At 4 A. M. Lt. Carl Law reported by radio that he and 15 men were through the minefield.

"He said the Gut was surrounded by a thick stone wall and they could find no entrance. He said there were about 10 German machine guns dug in outside of the wall and that prisoners claimed there were a hundred Germans defending the Gut.

"We sent the Second Platoon under Lt. Proffitt into the minefield to help Lieutenant Law but they also ran into mines. Lieutenant Proffitt and his sergeant were disabled and the platoon was withdrawn. As the men were working their way out of the minefield I saw a man explode a mine and go down. An aid man and a rifleman went toward him and the rifleman tripped a mine and was blown to bits. The aid man got the injured man, gave him first aid,

---

[1] 29, Let's Go, Ibid

returned and sent two litter bearers toward him. The litter bearers tripped a mine and both were killed."

George Company claimed it reached its objective at the Hasenfeld Gut in its morning report of December 6. In truth, the company was so exhausted and so weak from lack of functioning manpower that it just stopped--short of occupying the area, but driving the Germans out.

Also in truth, I don't remember much about lying in cold mud and shooting. I remember it was half-raining, half-snowing. I know we called for our artillery and I remember the Heini position was blasted, less than 200 yards from me. I felt those rounds, too, but like the Heinis, just bored myself deep into the mud. Thank God, none of them were short; we didn't have holes like the Germans.

There was no way to lead troops in suicidal situations like that one. We backed out, but so did the Germans. We withdrew before dawn, probably a sorry excuse for an attacking force. We were finished. We just walked away. I was like everyone else, simply drained, shivering, wet and spiritless sick.

Our sister regiment, the 115th, was called in to help and finally cleared the Gut area and the entire west bank during the next few days. Later, we were officially relieved by the 115th and sent back to Schaufenberg, 15 miles to the rear, for reorganization and refitting. It was time. George Company was down to a total of 63 not-very-effective men. That was one-third of our normal operating strength.

Our experienced troops were as close to a breakdown then as I've ever known. I was reminded of the old truism, "the longer you fight a war the more you figure your number is coming up and that feeling, at one time, gets to be God-awful. The best soldiers are guys with no experience who are more amazed than frightened."

And again, it's startling what a few days of non-stress rest, showers and warm food will do for young men. Recovery time is quick, as it was for George Company that December--after we got out of the cold mud.

We were still in that recovery mode--I went to Holland with some of our troops for a pre-Christmas dance put on by the somewhat bored and not young ladies of Kerkrade on the night of December 15--when the Battle of the Bulge, Hitler's giant counteroffensive some 30 miles to our south, broke on the morning of December 16.

The Division missed most of the Ardennes fighting, but we never knew until after the war, when German documents were reviewed, how close the Blue and Gray came to being the point of attack.

7

The Battle FOR the Bulge

*I learned to shoot left-handed; it didn't
make much difference because there
wasn't much to shoot at*

The great German counteroffensive of December, 1944, popularly known as the Battle of the Bulge, proved Jerry could still fight effectively. It also proved the worth of the American combat soldier. Even though thousands surrendered, many more thousands fought on in individual and small unit delaying actions--undirected by any headquarters--and under the most miserable winter conditions imaginable.

During the weeks preceding the breakout, the Germans had massed 24 divisions and supporting troops in a small sector of the Eifel Hills near Belgium's Ardennes Forest, all of this somehow unknown to and unrecognized by First Army intelligence.

I don't believe this assembly of tanks and manpower could have happened in front of the 29th Division positions without us suspecting. By early December, we were sending nightly patrols to the Roer River bank just to listen for tank motors and movement on the enemy side. Reports were detailed and complete, particularly if the patrols even thought they heard something. I know, because I was often part of these information-gathering forays.

In fact, our sector of the Roer River front was almost as lightly held as the Ardennes sector. We had three divisions in the XIX Corps, the Blue and Gray, the 30th and the 2nd Armored. And we were getting ready to attack on a relatively narrow front when the Battle of the Bulge broke, affecting the American lines from the Ninth Army's furthermost north unit, our 29th Division, through the entire Third Army to the south, also just getting ready to launch an attack.

The Germans thrust a broad, 75-mile-wide wedge against four First Army divisions--the 106th, 4th and 28th Infantry plus a good part of the 9th Armored Division. Within hours those divisions were destroyed as cohesive, controlled fighting units. And within a few more hours, rumors were all over Allied rear areas, where panic seemed to own a magic grab.

Even behind our XIX Corps, there was gunfire and what someone at the time called "gross instability." What set off our backcourt supporters were rumors that whole battalions of English-speaking German paratroopers had been dropped for sabotage purposes. As usual with wartime stories, this one was greatly exaggerated; our anti-aircraft defenses did shoot down a planeload of paratroopers at Aldenhoven in the early morning hours of December 17, and Colonel Skorzeny did get a few jeep loads of his Germans disguised as Americans through the Ardennes lines in the early confusion. Most of these specially-trained, English-speaking Germans were killed or captured; in any event, they did no great damage. Their main mission was to misdirect traffic. Some of the rumors had Skorzeny's men going to Paris to assassinate General Eisenhower.

Bogeymen are easy to create in wartime situations, and I've noted that their creation is not confined to the battlefield. The most fertile grounds for these stories are in supply dumps or rear echelon motor pools. Give a story wheels and it will go most anywhere.

One thing the counteroffensive did for us, however, was to cause some of our Division service units, such as the finance office under Lt. Col. Louis Lucas, to organize defense battalions and require refresher lessons in basic infantry combat.

On December 17, a day after the Heini thrust, the 30th Division was ordered out of our attack line and sent to the Bulge defense. Another three days and the 2nd Armored left, too. The 29th took over their positions and the scheduled attack on the Roer was postponed.

It would actually be February before we crossed the river in strength, three months after our arrival in the area and nearly three months behind our schedule to clear German troops from the entire west bank of the Rhine River, another 40 to 50 miles beyond the Roer.

It wasn't only the Bulge which caused a delay in our attack. The Roer River was controlled by seven large German dams located near the Hurtgen Forest directly south of our position. We dared not cross the Roer at our location because of the good chance our advance units would be cut off if and when the Germans released water in the dams, creating a raging flood and destroying bridges on our backside.

While the Blue and Gray did not participate directly in the Bulge, we certainly were interested and affected observers.

German documents reviewed after the war proved that the Wehrmacht's generals favored striking the Allies through the Roer River flatlands and likely between the Blue and Gray and the British regiment on our left (the Germans loved to hit on division, corps or army control borders, figuring more confusion could result, and attacking on a boundary between American and British forces would even be a multiplier). The German generals also obviously favored open country for their attacking Panzers.

In fact, the only reason most historians could uncover for the attack through the Ardennes was that Hitler personally picked the time and the place. This was the same terrain used as a launching pad for his hugely-successful 1940 invasion of the low countries and France. Otherwise it made no military sense to try to mount a swift-moving attack through difficult terrain in the wintertime. Unless there was complete surprise. . .

Not only did our intelligence fail to pick up the troop and equipment concentrations but they also failed to realize who was handling German strategy. If, as they thought, they were facing traditional German generalship, then they would expect a large-scale counter attack to occur only after the Americans had substantially penetrated the Fatherland. Either flank of a finger-like advance would be vulnerable.

When Hitler fired his by-the-book Army leader, Field Marshal von Rundstedt, some months earlier and then brought him back as a figurehead leader for this offensive, smart people on the Allied side should have suspected that they were then dealing with an unstable and egomaniacal Hitler and not the predictable von Rundstedt or his generals.

The Bulge was a madman's dream, it's true. On December 12, just four days before the push, Hitler spoke to his generals. Playing on every emotion, he declared: "You can't extract enthusiasm and self-sacrifice like something tangible and bottle and preserve them. They are generated just once in the course of a revolution, and will gradually die away. The grayness of the day and the conveniences of life will then take hold on men again and turn them into solid citizens in gray flannel suits."[1] Whatever passed for his generalship, Hitler had insight into character.

General Bradley left his headquarters in Belgium the day of the attack and didn't really hear about it until that evening, when he arrived at Ike's headquarters near Paris. General Hodges of the First Army and his VIII Corps commander, General Troy Middleton (he was also in charge of the Brest campaign) heard advance reports of Ardennes activity by the Germans but both dismissed it and took no action until the enemy was 10 to 15 miles inside the American defenses.

General Ike was one of the first of the Allied commanders to recognize the potential severity of the threat. He was meeting with Bradley that evening in Versailles on the need for more infantry combat

[1] *Hitler's Last Gamble*, by Jacques Nobecourt, Shocken Books, N.Y.

replacements. An aid handed Ike a note about the attack, and he suggested to Bradley that maybe he ought to send General Middleton some help, stating "This is more than a localized attack. It isn't logical for the German to begin a local attack at our weakest point."

General Eisenhower had a similar counterattack situation at Kassarine Pass in Tunisia in 1942. German Field Marshal Rommel, acknowledged on both sides as a prime strategist, attacked a weakly-held area while the Allies were massing men and equipment for an attack in another sector. Ike, according to biographers, had nightmares that this would be repeated.[2] He was right, only this time it was Hitler's limited military experience directing the show rather than Rommel's genius. And that's probably why the Germans neglected their big opportunity to curl back to the north, after their initial penetration, to hit the rear of the U. S. First and Ninth Armies. German troops were ordered by Hitler to keep going west until they crossed the Meuse River, deep in Belgium, and then shoot for Brussels and Antwerp.

This is much too ambitious a plan for the manpower and resources we have, the German generals told Hitler.[1] The Fuhrer remained cantankerous, stubborn and unpredictable. He insisted that they keep going west until they ran out of fuel. After all, he probably reasoned, "we did this well before--in 1940."

In *A Time for Trumpets,* Charles MacDonald wrote:

"Along with Field Marshal Walter Model, von Runstedt proposed another solution: Attack from the north into the northern flank of the Ninth Army (the 29th Division) which on November 16 had commenced a major offensive in the Aachen sector (Ed. note: actually, it was a bit north of Aachen, in the flatlands leading to the Roer River) but failed to achieve a breakthrough. This maneuver then posed a chance to destroy some 14 American divisions weakened by their offensive and thereby set up an opportunity to go for Hitler's large reach for Antwerp later."

Von Runstedt kept trying to change Hitler's mind,

---

[2] Ibid

[1] *The Second World War,* by Martin Gilbert, Henry Holt & Co.

along with Model, Generals Manteufel and Sepp Deitrich, who said at the time: 'All Hitler wants me to do is to cross a river, capture Brussels, then go on and take Antwerp. All this in the worst time of the year through the Ardennes where the snow is waist deep and there isn't room to deploy four tanks abreast, let alone armored divisions. And where it doesn't get light until 8 and it gets dark again at 4 and with reformed divisions made up of kids and sick old men--and at Christmas.'[1]

One German commander, after his attack briefing, was asked for his estimate on the chances for success.

"Ten to 20 percent," he said.

"Good enough. We go," Field Marshal Model is reported to have replied.

German General Kraemer, Chief of Staff, had this to say about Hitler's attack concept. [2] *"Es ist toll! Dummes Unternehen!"* (It's crazy. What a lunatic operation.)

Two of the U. S. divisions defending the Ardennes were veteran but exhausted outfits. The 4th and the 28th Divisions had just gone through the costly Hurtgen Forest campaign. Our former assistant division commander, Norman (Dutch) Cota, the 29th's D-Day hero, was now commanding general of the 28th. This was a Pennsylvania national guard outfit with a brilliant red keystone for an identification patch. We called it the Bucket of Blood patch and the 28th proved it at Hurtgen.

The 4th had landed on D-Day at Utah Beach and served well since. Only the 3rd Division, which started in Africa and Italy and later led the invasion of southern France, and the 4th had more total World War II casualties than the 29th. And many of the 4th's casualties came at Hurtgen, less than a month before the Bulge.

New and untried units defending the Ardennes included the 106th Infantry Division and the 9th Armored. Bordering the 106th on the north was the 99th Division, part of another corps. It was almost as green as the 106th. The 14th Cavalry Group, a mechanized outfit, also had part of the front and was basically untested, too.

---

[1] The Battle for the Ardennes, Ibid

[2] *Hitler's Last Gamble*, Ibid

These units were arrayed much the same as we were--advance outposts connected by frequent patrols with main defense lines several thousand yards back. Perhaps they were a bit more relaxed; the Ardennes was supposed to be a rest and recuperation sector.

Each unit had its own small reserve force, all located within a mile or two of the so-called front. Everything depended on good communications between the front and rear and with neighboring units under different command--and that is where the Americans were and always have been most vulnerable. Heavy shelling prior to the German attack eliminated many American field unit telephone lines, (radio was less reliable then) drastically impairing communications. Consequently, each small unit ended up doing what its platoon leader or captain thought best.

The Germans understandably attacked on unit boundaries, as they did December 16 between the 99th of V Corps and the 106th of VII Corps. That pathway turned into a primary route through the American lines. But the whole area was thinly manned with new and/or tired soldiers, supposedly refitting, replacing and training.

Yet it was this same combination of new and tired G. I.'s who saved this country's bacon at the close of 1944.

No matter what, the American combat soldier didn't give up easily, the Germans found. The typical G. I. during those early days of the Bulge had no contact or communication with headquarters--or generally with anyone except his squad or platoon leader. He had no food, sometimes little or no ammunition. It was shivering wet and cold, often snowing. Yet he kept fighting. He slowed the German attack; his stubbornness eventually stalled the entire Kraut offensive.

The Germans took a total of 15,000 prisoners during the Bulge. But two-thirds of these didn't surrender until December 19 and 20, nearly four days after the battle's start, when they were basically abandoned in below freezing temperatures for more than 72 hours, with no orders, no food and water and likely, little ammunition. The heroism of these small units, each resisting the German counteroffensive independently, allowed time to organize the defenses of Bastogne and other key points further west. And it wasn't just infantry this time. The defense groups included artillerymen without their cannons, quartermasters without their trucks--but everybody, including cooks, with a rifle!

Of the 600,000 Americans involved in the Bulge, there were 81,000 casualties, including 19,000 killed. The British, employing 55,000 men, lost 1,400 of which 200 were killed. The Germans used 500,000 men and lost at least 100,000 of these--killed, wounded or captured. Both sides lost about 800 tanks each and the German lost more than 1,000 planes.[1] The Americans could replace the lost hardware in a few weeks; the Germans, never.

Up north, we were having our troubles, too. On December 16, opening day of the Bulge attack, we were the targets of a couple of air attacks in addition to heavy shelling. That day we took nine bombing and strafing raids and that night we were hit 19 more times. Jerry meant to keep us in our holes.

We had good reason to believe we were the next big counteroffensive target, but nothing happened over a day or two, then nothing happened over a week. We waited, always on alert, listening for the other shoe to drop. It never happened.

The biggest success of the Battle of the Bulge from the German side was the near-panic created in American rear areas. Whenever we went back to the coal mine building in Alsdorf, our division showering point, we were challenged frequently for the password. Everybody now carried a gun whether they knew how to use it or not. Personally, I thought we may have faced greater danger in Alsdorf than on the line.

Holland, less than 30 miles away, was really our rest center. It, too, was cold and wet and muddy. But it was much better than Germany where we never saw any civilians, although I'm sure they were in the same neighborhoods. This was fine with us. Civilians in a combat area are never welcome, even if they're friendly.

---

[1] *A Time for Trumpets*, Charles MacDonald, William Morrow & Co.

It kept getting colder, at least it seemed so to me. Right after December 16th it began snowing and the white flakes kept coming. By the 20th, when we moved back to Koslar to take over our old, but much larger, defense responsibilities, foot-deep snow covered most of the ugliness and ground gashes. I was actually happy to be back in the old railroad station.

Every day around noon we would take a few shells from the Germans. They always stopped after a dozen or so rounds and they never hit anything while I was there. After a day of non-movement, our guys were anxious for darkness so they could walk to company headquarters and pick up their first--and only--hot meal of the day.

We also had to man the company outposts on the river and to send out patrols to contact those posts and other neighboring units. None of us had enough men to hold that sector if an attack were ever mounted, and we knew it. Again George Company was on the Division's flank, this time on the left. Our contact to our left was the British Second Army. The Limeys were the better part of a mile away, but it was always a pleasure to visit them. They still had Scotch.

Christmas came and went. Everybody had turkey and the trimmings and everybody got a present, whether their families sent them something or not. Division distributed small gifts to those who had been overlooked. I thought that was a great touch, although most of us shared whatever we received from the states. I remember my special gift from Iowa was a box of Divinity candy, a white fudge-like substance that I dearly loved. This batch arrived a little hard, but that didn't seem to bother me or the others who sampled it. All in all, it was a good Christmas--certainly much better than our buddies to the south had. The weather remained miserable.

I remember taking out a patrol the night of Christmas Day. It was generally just a walk around Koslar, but there was some artillery coming in every few minutes. I hit the ground when it blasted and I hurried through the streets and outskirts fields, I remember that.

Maybe it is true that a person, once wounded, becomes less effective in combat situations. More likely, he becomes super-cautious. I just know I wasn't the same troop leader I was in France. Hopefully, the men didn't notice too big a difference--then again, how could they? Except for a couple, they weren't the same men.

In those days we were mostly living in cellars and eating German potatoes. I even had them raw one time. For Christmas we did manage a few homemade decorations. But I distinctly remember the Germans were singing from their side of the river. Done with the help of loudspeakers, the carols sounded great--even in German. Quite a few were done in English--in fact, most. And there were some beautiful German originals, most always followed by some Kraut propaganda about why were we there this season when we could be home with our families? The songs did create memories but no deserters.

More snow came just after Christmas and it turned cold, the kind of cold where the snow crunches and squeaks beneath boots--the same kind of below-zero cold I used to know in Northern Iowa. And it didn't get better. As in Iowa, once it started to get cold in Germany it hung on for a week or two.

By New Year's Eve I realized I had never been so cold for so long. It was affecting my hand which had turned an ugly red and streaked purple. Moving the fingers was difficult. I practiced shooting left-handed and actually was proud of my marksmanship. I probably wasn't as quick left-handed, but the ability to shoot fast is only a small part of good soldiering anyway.

There wasn't much happening in our part of Germany right then, but we knew the lull was only temporary. We saw our objective daily--or rather nightly-- a group of burned out, shelled buildings on the high-ground horizon. This was Julich, entrance to the industrial Rhineland.

We saw much of the city built on the river bluffs regularly on our patrols throughout December. The scattered and mostly-wrecked houses on the German side still had lights. Occasionally we saw their inhabitants, probably soldiers but we couldn't tell in the darkness. They were wandering about and talking, laughing.

I got my share of these patrols because I could

speak (understand is a better word for it) a little German. I took two years of the language in high school which was a long way away right then.

Our pattern was mostly the same; we would go to the river bank around 9 or 10 at night, sit and listen until nearly midnight and come home and report. Any unusual sounds, such as heavy motor and tank transport, came first. Then any understandable talk or movement. These patrols were what we called "hear-ye" excursions.

Some of our patrols became raiding parties where we would cross the river and try to capture prisoners. I drew one of these in early January. A half-dozen of us were to cross the river in rubber boats and scout a route to a castle on the high ground on the other side of Julich. This was not as difficult a job as it sounded at first. The Krauts, we knew from repeated earlier forays, let us explore a bit on their side of the river so long as we did not ruin their sleep. But there was no guarantee. One of these nights, I and others firmly believed, they were going to turn on their fiery furnace of welcome.

We got to our river departure point in good shape, but when we tried to put the rubber boats in the partially-frozen Roer River, some of our men slipped and fell through the shore ice.

Evidently this was the night they were waiting for. Our noise brought all hell from the German side. Flares first, then mortars and artillery, not to mention some spraying machine gun and rifle fire. We ducked into the snow behind trees; the shelling was brief. When it stopped I checked around and miraculously no one was hit. But we had awakened the giant. Probably it was a good thing for us that the Germans exploded their fly-in-the-web intentions early.

I debated with myself only briefly. There wasn't anything else we could do now--so we left that area in a hurry.

Later I explained to an intelligence officer that it was impossible in that launch area not to make noise because of the river's flimsy shelf ice and uneven terrain, plus snow cover where no one is certain where he is stepping. Division didn't send any rifle platoon patrols across the river after that--at least until I left in mid-

January. But aggressive patrolling continued. It was part of our heritage.

On January 3 we moved from Koslar to Merzenhausen, a little more than a mile to the north. We took over the defensive positions of Charlie Company. The foxholes and the cellar positions were already there; we just vaulted into them under light artillery fire.

It was very difficult to keep busy or to think positively under these circumstances--cold, miserable climate; an aggressive enemy popping shells at you every time you move and the worst situation of all--that of forever waiting. There was also the factor which I termed the unknown. Most of us believed we would be extremely lucky personally to survive another patrol, another shelling or just another freezing snowfall. Somehow we always did.

The biggest concern to American troops then was the ever-present Heini mine. The Germans were great sowers of minefields. They knew the paralyzing fear effect of these blasters on the G. I.'s so they continued to put up their signs *Achtung Minen!* regardless of whether or not there were any mines around.

And even when an army is equipped properly for the weather--and this was rare, indeed, in those days--it probably suffers more casualties from nature than it does from the enemy. Our frost-bitten hands and feet casualties were enormous. Just plain disease caused by living conditions can be paralyzing, too. Our situation in Europe during the winter of 1944-45 certainly came under that category.

I kept my injured right hand in a big, hand-made mitten most of the time. Remembering what the doctors told me, I used it as much as I could. It never hurt until I tried to make a fist, which became more difficult as the cold weather continued.

George Company was gradually building its strength again by early January. The roster was down to 84 just before Christmas. By mid-January we were at 117. We all knew what the build-up was for.

Life in occupied Germany was not easy that winter. Mostly, we kept to our own small groups. I didn't get the platoon together very often; there was no need. I was sort of in a blue funk as I believe most of our people were. I guess we needed some action--and I got it that second week of January, 1945.

8

Final Days and Nights

*That cold, deserted street became my Midnight
of the Soul--a time of total breakdown,
even of survival instincts*

*M*y last act of war with the Blue and Gray was
anything but impassioned; some observers might call it a
simple matter of hauling the obvious wreck off to the
junkyard.

Our front was actually a sideshow during my final
days with the 29th. The main event was in the Ardennes
just to our south. By early January, however, the outcome
of that Bulge eruption was confirmed in favor of the Allies
and the mop up was beginning.

There was a stirring in our area by the end of the
first week in January--increased patrolling, rehearsals of
river crossings, narrowing the front and, above all, a
renewed attitude of attack. Americans, I'm convinced, are
not suited to a defensive situation and really don't care for
it. Mention attack and morale perks up immediately.

General Gerhardt understood the lure of attack for
his 29th Division G. I.'s. His role was something of a
cheerleader's, keeping us charged up for our "final run at
the Hun." His answer in early January was to increase
patrolling activity. Some of us thought he probably was

disappointed that we weren't down in the Ardennes fixing up that scene, so he figured we could do penance by sending out more patrols to stir up some activity on our front.

Patrolling wasn't easy. Some people, myself included, would rather be in an aggressive attack situation where we at least had the Krauts on their heels, reacting to our moves. Patrols generally operated in enemy territory on enemy terms. Particularly was this true in our situation. Aside from the lousy weather and even worse ground conditions, there were the mines. Each day and most of the nights the Germans would sneak over the Roer and distribute more anti-personnel mines on the routes we generally used to get to the river. They delighted, I'm sure, in spreading wire concertinas, or bundles of barbed wire, in approaches where they didn't have mines. They would then festoon the wire with tin cans, war junk of all sorts and really anything that would make a noise when somebody touched it.

Then they sat back several hundred yards away with their heavy weapons and waited for the noise. Previously zeroed-in artillery and mortars became killer instruments when the Heinis touched firing buttons. If an American patrol ever got caught in one of these binds, say good bye to a good many of its members.

Where the Germans didn't have their obstacles they generally had mines--or their *Achtung Minen* signs. We never knew which areas were actually mined and we had no hankering to find out.

I drew a "listening" and "capture-if-you-can" patrol assignment the night of January 13. I took a squad from my platoon, plus two more BAR (Browning Automatic Rifle) teams for a total of 12 men. Our job was to get to the river, scout for any sign of enemy activity including German patrols who may be distributing mines or laying wire. Unless we had direct orders to the contrary, we weren't likely to bring back any prisoners from Heini mine-laying groups--they were dead if we saw them. This time we had orders to take a few prisoners if we could. I knew I would have my hands full to prevent shooting in case we ran into mine planters.

The patrol started down a snow-covered turnip field but it was so slow going in the sloppy field I elected to use both sides of a nearby road--using both sides in case we had to jump into the ditches in a hurry.

None of us looked forward to that solution. The ditches were filled with snow and ice, some in-process-of freezing water and mud, possibly mines and certainly other war junk I didn't want to know anything about. But I thought we would be a little less visible to Jerry from the dark background of the road. The turnip field was white; I'm sure we would have been easily picked-up black dots moving on a field of white had we stayed in the field.

As I understood it, it was only later that our outfit got white camouflage clothing. Most German units had white outfits from the start of winter warfare.

Our patrol had an advantage or two. The night was dark. Incoming shells hitting in the soft fields tended to implode, causing little damage to anyone more than a few steps away.

The road, however, was my choice--and down it we went, mostly unmolested and relatively fast. We were approaching the river area and I had just decided to leave the blacktop when it came--the heavy hiss of a flare launching.

I held up both arms, our signal to freeze in place, crouched if we had time. Hopefully, the Krauts would miss us--but they didn't. Within seconds in came the mortars. There was always a lighter hissing or whistling sound before they hit. The flare's light was dying but it was too late now. After the first shells exploded I hollered "hit it!" and I suspect everyone dove for the ditches--I know I did.

I got up after the first few rounds had blasted the road and surrounding fields, knowing that we had to get out of that zone. I started running down the road toward the river, shouting "Let's move it!" My sergeant, at the rear of the patrol, got the others moving, too.

I stopped a hundred or so yards down the road, moved to a wooded area to the left and waited for the rest of the patrol. They came in, breathless, a few minutes later and we counted heads.

Everyone was there--a minor miracle. I may have

been the only casualty. I had felt a sharp pain in my right knee area when I was hitting the ditch. Now I saw a tear in the pant leg and some blood coming out of a gash on the outside of the knee. Nothing serious. The knee was functioning. I may just have hit it on a sharp stone or a stray piece of metal laying in the ditch.

Scouts went out to report to our outpost and get a safe route down to the river. We had to wait only a few minutes before they returned, and we then started to move slowly forward. I sent our BAR teams out to our flanks. Every few yards we stopped to listen. Nothing.

It was still early--a little after 2100 hours. We should stay at least another hour, maybe two.

But I didn't know if we could manage that. My knee probably was bothering me more mentally than physically, although it was still bleeding and starting to stiffen. My concern mainly involved the snow dunking all of us took in the road ditches. It was terribly cold and we were all at least partially wet. I even heard teeth chattering, several groans and complaints that "only in the Army could a man sit in sub-freezing temperatures, wet to the skin, and nobody did anything about it."

I figured we could take it only for another 20 to 30 minutes, if we could stay reasonably quiet for that time. Everybody took turns moving around. It was the only way we could stay functional.

I sent two of the remaining men up the river on a scouting expedition, telling them to go as far as they could, quietly, but to return in 15 minutes. The rest of us set up a perimeter defense and waited. The BAR teams were still on our flanks and we were secure. I decided we could wait only the 15 minutes without endangering everyone on the patrol. Within a relatively short time I would lose most of the efficiency of this group, if I hadn't lost it already.

My upriver pair returned within the 15 minutes. No activity. We made it back to the outpost station without trouble. We then took off for home, over the fields this time. No more incoming. Everybody just fell out when we reached the company area, eager to get to something warm.

I went in to report after examining the knee carefully. It didn't seem to be bad; I had either taken a grazing shell fragment or ripped it on something razor sharp. I couldn't stop the bleeding. It hurt bad, even worse than my hand. I was a mess.

My report was verbal, to either a company or battalion staffer--I think the latter. And I was hurting, both physically and mentally. I think I told the guy there was no way I was going to risk the entire patrol by staying a full hour or more; yes, I had had it personally and I was going to the aid station, if I could get there. The combination of cold and hurt and frustration was getting to me. No, I didn't need any help. I probably didn't even complete the report--I had to get out of there before I broke down. Up the stairs and again out into the bitter night. To the aid station, was all I could think.

As I limped down that deserted, cold and snow-encrusted street in the blackened ruins of a German town, by now cradling my swelling hand, I began to cry. Too much, I moaned to myself, too much for this soldier.

It became a piled-on, uncontrollable outburst for several minutes. I stopped and then, for some reason or other, sank face down on a pile of dirt and snow, waves of self-pity now rolling through my mind and over my body. Nothing was going right. I couldn't even complete a patrol. I wanted to float away, to sleep, but I was too sore. The knee hurt. My right hand was nearly useless. I started to shake and the reaction kept up, stronger by the minute. My mind was racing to all the black conclusions--it was the Midnight of my Soul. . . .the darkness, the hopelessness of it all. I blubbered, sobbed and probably even howled my grief into the night. Flashes of thoughts--maybe it was time for me to check out. Maybe I shouldn't even try anymore. I wasn't helping anybody, least of all myself. Then I thought of a simple bullet suicide, but no, I probably would louse that up, too. Then more stabs of the hopelessness of it all.

I wondered what the next trip out would be--and the next and the next. Do people like me lose it all? Do we all turn into shivering, frightened shells? Too involved with our own fears and thoughts? More calmly now. . Why, for example, did I leave early tonight? I should have stayed but I didn't only because this lieutenant was more concerned about himself than his mission.

Then I just lay there, on that dirty snowbank, heaving and sobbing. There was a time--I have no idea how long I was there, no one came along or bothered me-- when I slid to the bottom of the pile and into the street's gutter. I must have curled up to a fetal position. It was cold. That's what finally woke me up to where I was--I staggered to my feet because the cold was actually painful. Some lights were shining, and I dimly saw the aid station only a couple of blocks away. Shivering and miserable, I made my slow way to the station and back to warmth and life.

Since that night many years ago I've often thought what might have happened had I never struggled on. Probably not much. Somebody likely would have found me the next day, bent and frozen. He may even have remarked that it was too bad the lieutenant couldn't have made it to the aid station, only a few steps away.

I remember I was so determined to get to help that by the time I reached the station I had stopped the tears. I was dragging the leg, simply a numb shell intent on one thing--getting to the aid station.

A medic quickly put something on the knee plus a bandage, looked at my right hand and suggested I come in to see Captain Herter tomorrow. He also gave me a couple of pills which he said would calm me down. By that time I had recovered my military mind and actually thought I only needed something to keep me going until the next morning. Staying in the aid station that night was not really part of my plan, but I think that's what happened. I must have passed out. Or just gone to sleep. It was warm and sleep helps to forget.

In any event, I was still a bit of a basket case when I saw Herter the next morning. He looked me over and asked me one question: "Do you shoot right handed?"

Once, I replied, adding that I was using the left hand now.

He shook his head and said he was sending me back to Liege, Belgium, to an Army Group hospital where they could examine the hand. He was concerned because

Here's what's left of Julich after we crossed the Roer, seen at the top of the photo beyond the infamous Citadel, its massive walls surrounded by what's left of a moat.

-Photo from *29 Let's Go*

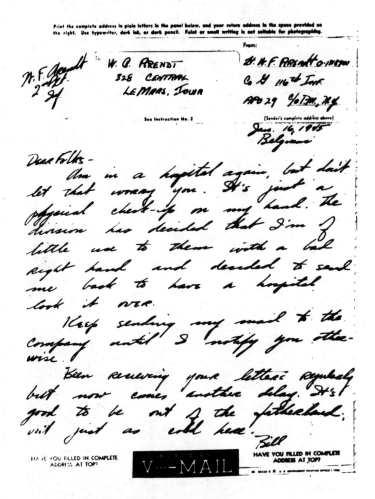

V-Mail was normally the easiest and quickest way to correspond with America. Here's one of mine, written after my second hospitalization. For some unexplained reason, this was delayed several weeks. Regular letters from close relatives in the service were the only way folks at home escaped worry. All of our mail home was censored by officers within the unit not to reveal location, action and unit.

of the swelling, color and possible lack of circulation due to the cold weather.

"If we were in Puerto Rico, no worry," he smiled.

He barely looked at the knee, but he did put a fresh bandage on it, plus giving me some more sulfa.

I never did find out whether I was wounded a second time that night, and to tell the truth, I didn't much care. At least I was going back to where it was warm. With buildings. Captain Herter told me to report for transport later in the morning. He told me to keep the hand close to my body for warmth.

I went back to the company and said my good byes, not reluctantly but, hopefully, not too pridefully either. I think I was still a little teared up, always when I said good bye to the platoon members I could catch. I hugged a couple of sergeants, especially Perkins, and predicted I would be back in a week.

Secretly, I hoped I would never see this again. They wished me luck and some of them even congratulated me on finding a way out. Yeah, I replied, and minus a hand. I felt guilty again about leaving and turned teary. Then I left in a hurry.

If there ever was such a problem as combat fatigue, I had in my last 24 hours with George Company. Later, I read an interesting report on the subject by the Office of the U. S. Surgeon General:

"The simple fact that the danger of being killed or maimed imposes a strain so great that it causes men to break down. One look at the shrunken, apathetic faces of psychiatric patients as they come stumbling into the medical station, sobbing, trembling, referring shatteringly to 'them shells' and to buddies mutilated or dead is enough to convince most observers of this fact.

"There's no such thing as 'getting used to' combat. Each man 'up there' knows that at any moment he may be killed, a fact kept constantly before his mind by the sight of dead or wounded buddies around him. Each moment of combat imposes a strain so great that men will break down in direct relation to the intensity or duration of their exposure. Thus, psychiatric casualties are as inevitable as gunshot or shrapnel wounds in warfare."

American forces estimated that a man could last in

a mentally sound condition for about 200 regimental combat days. These were not successive days of patrolling, attacking or defending, just a total number of exposure days, even in reserve, before warning signs should go up.

British troops were pulled out of combat every 12 days, regardless, and were given an automatic four days rest before they were recommitted to the front lines. The Brits figured their men could go a little more than a year in combat with this type of schedule. Then an extended period of rest was called for.

Of the two systems I would much prefer that of the British, recognizing that there may be some situations in which the 12 days could become 15 or 20 days, but no more.

Hysteria in battle came much faster if troops were drawn tight emotionally for extended periods, such as in the Battle of the Bulge. General Matthew Ridgway, then commanding our airborne, gave this example:

"We were in a situation where the Germans had brought up some flat trajectory guns and were shelling our little group unmercifully. Fragments whizzed everywhere. One struck our artillery observer. A second struck his jeep. As the shell struck, an infantry sergeant standing nearby became hysterical. He threw himself into a ditch by the side of the road, crying and raving, screaming.

"I walked over to try to calm him, tried talking, tried to help him get ahold of himself, but it had no effect. He remained crouched in the ditch, cringing with terror. So I called my jeep driver and told him to take this man to the nearest M.P. and if started to escape, shoot him without hesitation. I reasoned that if any American soldier had seen him in this condition it would be the end of morale for that soldier and his group."

General Ridgway comtinued: "It is an appalling thing to witness--to see a man break completely like that in battle. It's worse than watching a death, for you are seeing something more important than a body die. You are seeing the death of a man's spirit, of his pride, of all that gives meaning and purpose to life."

---

[1] *The Taste of Courage,* by Flowers and Reeves, Harper & Row

The American army in Europe in the winter of 1944-45 had little choice in assigning combat infantry forces. Commitments to cover a front line from Holland to the Alps exceeded the manpower available.

David Eisenhower, writing in his *Eisenhower at War*, said: "The typical American division north of the Ardennes on November 20 was at 70 percent of its combat strength. Losses in the November offensive totaled 64,000. Yet Washington cut replacement troops to Europe from 80,000 to 64,000 (in that period), the balance going to the Pacific."

We probably got the slapping around we deserved in the Battle of the Bulge. But why were we overextended? Because we got into campaigns of attrition, like the Hurtgen Forest, the Roer River flatlands, even Brest. All of them consumed too much combat manpower for their strategic importance. But that's in hindsight, of course.

It was late in the morning when we got started to the Army hospital in Liege. I was talking to no one, paying little attention to anything other than keeping my hand, plus the rest of my body, warm. We jeeped it back to Division headquarters, then transferred to the ever-present army truck. It was less than 100 miles to Liege from our Division Rear areas. And even though the Bulge had stabilized by mid-January, the rear echelon was still security conscious. I guess that was good, but to me that day was mostly annoying. We must have been stopped a half dozen times and routed in circles even more often.

It took us the rest of the day to get to Liege; in fact it was dark when we pulled up to a rambling pile of brick sitting atop one of the many hills in that historic cathedral and museum city in eastern Belgium.

I was assigned to a bed. I dropped my musette bag--that was all I had, not even a change of clothes--and headed for the door. No one was going to stop me.

I was looking for a ride into town, mainly to see some intact buildings--and people--for a change. I was anticipating having a warm drink in a warm bar with some hopefully warm Belgians.

Getting the ride was no problem. Actually, we

cruised the streets of downtown Liege that evening in an engineer's jeep, the engineer captain at the wheel. We didn't see a soul. Finally, three or four of us piled out at a hotel, only to find that it was occupied by our First Army headquarters troops. They weren't interested in our problem of finding civilian companionship. We eventually went back to the hospital cots. At least it was better than what I had in Germany.

The Krauts' V-1 buzz bombs were dropping into Liege at that time, although at a lesser rate than during the Bulge, I was told. For most of us, they were nothing to worry about. We had seen worse where we came from.

But the bombs did bother the locals--and they truly were scary when their motors stopped. There was a 10 second poignant pause and then a thunderclap explosion. A building, or in some cases an entire residential block, had gotten it.

There was a story circulating in the hospital when I arrived. It seems the number of German prisoners being kept under guard in the basement was increasing as were the Americans being hospitalized on the upper floors. Buzz bombs were falling, and the hospitalized Americans figured the German prisoners ought to be the first to be exposed. So they managed to transfer the prisoners to the upper floors while the G. I.'s took to the basement--a much safer place in case a buzz bomb hit.

By that time I had developed a fatalist's attitude, so it didn't really make much difference to me where the bombs landed. I knew my chances were better in Liege than where I came from.

Liege was a frosty city that winter. I hit it at a bad time, I'm sure, but I couldn't escape the feeling that these people were waiting to see who won this war. They probably had both the German and American flags ready to hang out their windows, depending on who was marching in their streets.

It was only near my departure time, possibly a week later, that I found a suburban hangout of very worried and silent civilians--no young females, even tending bar. There was Belgian *Biere* and some form of Canadian whiskey. No Scotch. Little talk.

Doctors wasted no time in examining me. I believe we arrived on a Sunday, and they were poking and prodding the next day. The hand's condition was a big item, of course. I opened and closed, wiggled fingers and had grab strength tests. When warm, movement and strength was generally okay, I suppose, but they didn't like the looks of the hand.

Poor circulation was the verdict. X-rays followed and there they--and I, for the first time-- saw the scattered lead fragments spread from the wrist into the fingers. They agreed with the doctors in England--not worth the surgical risk of going after the fragments. The upshot of it all was a hearing scheduled on whether or not I would remain on full service.

By the end of the week the hearing was convened. It lasted only 10 to 20 minutes. There was a board of three doctors, as I recall. They ignored my knee, which was also red and swollen at the time, and asked the same right-handed use questions that I had answered before. I was then dismissed for a couple of minutes for them to discuss the case, I presume, and was called back to hear that I was being reclassified to limited service, unfit for further combat duty.

Just like that. I couldn't suppress a muzzled yelp. They laughed and one cautioned: "Don't figure you're going back to the states for ROTC duty on a college campus, Lieutenant. We're going to send you to the 9th Service Command in Paris and they'll find something for you to do over here."

I did hold back a second cheer, but my head was exploding. I was going to Paris! No more shooting or mud or cold!

Actually, I didn't go to Paris, but to Versailles, about 30 miles south of the city. A truckload of us left the next day. Because I was the only officer in the shipment, I had the responsibility to see that all of us arrived as ordered, to a "reppel depple" just north of Versailles. I was told it was formerly a large estate, complete with a baronial house.

I figured that I might have some missing men if I

told them we weren't going straight to the biggest
nightclub in Paris. In fact, as we got close to the city I
routed the truck to a by-pass, telling the G. I.'s that we
should be seeing the Eiffel Tower any moment. When we
stopped at the country estate the army had taken over and
we unloaded, I told them the news: "This is your castle.
Paris is only 20 minutes away by inter-urban electric
railroad. You get passes from the commander's office--
over there," I pointed. The explanation worked. They
were as happy as I was to be anywhere near Paris.

We all bunked in a tent city on the estate grounds.
We really never stayed there, unless we were forced to
because of early commitments the following day. Passes to
Paris required only a request. And because all of the
replacements at this particular depot were headed away
from the action there was no need for close supervision.
We all went our way until someone called our number in
the form of an order to report to a new outfit.

My first days were spent mostly in Paris. It was a
thrill, even for this jaded G. I. I stood on the *Champs
Elysees*, just looking at people. I sat in a sidewalk cafe. I did
the entire tour bit, taking in every possible trip to historical
sites I could--Napoleon's tomb, the Louvre, the tower,
Place Concorde, the *Bois de Boulogne* and, of course, the *Arc
de Triomphe*. I even made the Left Bank and a few other
spots not so historic but perhaps more memorable. There
was no shortage of tourists, even in those wartime days.
Tour buses were filled, mostly with the military. But
gawkers of all vintages and nationalities--something that
still makes Paris unique--were everywhere.

I always found the French to have a haughty but
hearty culture. And I believe I know why. In a typical
Frenchman's opinion no civilization worthy of the name
can exist without some level of French input. The rest of
the world, they believe, is made up of savages, only a few
of which may be worth saving.

At the same time, the French are a lively, partying
people and, they most certainly would agree, with a sharp
and an aware culture featuring a magnificent history of
honoring individual freedoms. Maybe, if we think about
it, those freedoms are what we're all about. In my mind

they were mainly why we fought this war.

My poor college French found few takers in Paris. Parisians have their own version of the language anyway. I couldn't have understood them even if I'd taken 10 years of French courses.

Mostly, I toured Paris alone and was quite content to do so. There were too many Americans in uniform in Paris, I decided almost immediately. General Eisenhower never stinted on staff; I heard there were more than 100,000 people assigned to SHAEF (Supreme Headquarters, Allied Expeditionary Forces), but I can't really believe there wasn't a misplaced zero in that total. Still way too many. In any event, we uniformed Americans were stumbling over each other in Paris in the winter of 1945. We could have used a few more of these people in Germany, with rifles.

I tried to steer clear of headquarters types, figuring that if I avoided them they would miss seeing the chip on my shoulder and I might miss getting into trouble. In brief, my week in Paris was educational but a lonely-in-a-crowd time.

When orders came for my assignment to the Belgian Leave Section, headquartered in Brussels, I was ecstatic. It was early February and even though the days were misty and cold, I was more than ready to climb aboard another truck and move north through the gritty, dreary countryside of northern France and southern Belgium. Paris and Brussels are less than 250 miles apart, but again, it took us most of a long day to negotiate that distance.

We stopped in Lille, France, a steel and coal town not touched by the shells of war but just as surely gutted of its pride. Then it was up through the coal mining country of Walloon, or the southern, French-speaking half of Belgium. The same depressing scenes, including the black-lined, unsmiling faces.

Then I suddenly realized what was missing--young people. There were none I saw along the route. Even the young women kept out of view (I knew there must be some of these). Just tired, old and sour people in the industrial heartland of non-German Europe. It was another

learning chapter for me in the degradation of civilians who
were the victims of occupation and war.

    Brussels was the opening a new door. Like Paris, it
was bustling and busy, untouched by the war's violence
except for the toll on its younger people.
    After the misery I had seen earlier in the day,
Brussels was a fountain of joy. Many more people, looking
prosperous and sometimes smiling. A hard-working, clean
and cosmopolitan city, bi-lingual (French and Flemish)
with a good amount of English language understanding--
and maybe even friendly. People called it the "Little
Paris", but a city without the Parisian French arrogance. I
was going to find out.

9

The Delights of Brussels

*First happenings after I arrived in Brussels
were wild, something from dreams--
or even nightmares*

A sex-for-sale place, the Hotel Berger, was my first official quarters in Brussels. The Belgian Leave Section and American liaison units to British headquarters on the Continent billeted a dozen or more officers in its small but garish rooms, complete with *bidets* and balconies not far from busy *Avenue Louise*

I must say, however, the Berger was in an upscale area with no overt solicitations or *poules* parades. The hotel itself had a long history of a classy hot pillow joint where rooms were rented by the hour, particularly over the longish, three-hour lunch periods common in France and Belgium. Prime customers were Brussels businessmen who, with their female companions, had permanent reservation times certain days of the week. It was rare if any of these middle-aged Lotharios visited the Berger more than once a week.

It didn't take long for the Americans to find out what was going on. We all developed our favorites among the visiting ladies; I believe several of our chaps even approached them for dates after their dalliances at the Berger were concluded.

Make no mistake, however, Brussels was a tightly controlled British Army city. This was deep in Brit territory (the Americans had Paris in their sector). We Americans were guests in this city, as we were informed by our senior officers many times and by our hosts, but in the British subtle-sign way. No complaints from this Yank.

The American presence in Brussels was suffered only because of headquarters liaison functions and the Belgian Leave Section, a unique arrangement which would allow American combat troops three days vacation in a beautiful city basically untouched by war. And Brussels was not too far from the fighting in Germany, certainly much closer than Paris.

Our Belgian Leave Section was just getting started when I joined. We established an intake and discharge control center in *Place Cinquantenaire* in the heart of the city. All troops were to check in here and then be assigned to various hotels--actually most of them were downtown, about two or three dozen long blocks away from *Cinquantenaire*.

The same arrival trucks delivered the G.I.'s to their hotels and picked them up at the end of their stay. Everybody again was checked out through our control center and sent back to the war. In concept and practice, the program was one of the few R and R (Rest and Recuperation) ideas I saw which actually worked. And best of all, the G. I.'s loved it!

My first job with the BLS was running the intake-discharge center. We allowed the officer or sergeant in charge of an incoming truck to sign his load in and out, thus speeding the process considerably. I had up to a half-dozen G. I.'s working with me, plus liaison officers from various armies and services who were responsible for their people. Our headquarters was a series of large field hospital tents with long rows of tables inside.

We couldn't have designed a better spot for the intake/discharge center than the Belgians (and English) gave us. *Place Cinquantenaire* was dominated by a magnificent, nearly-four-story-tall series of Doric order columns and topped with house-sized statues of mounted grenadiers in battle or at full gallop. It commemorated

Belgium's fiftieth anniversary of freedom from the Dutch. The *Kaiskopfs* (literally, Cheeseheads in Flemish) were the last (not counting the recently-defeated Germans) of seven conquerors in the history of the *Belgae*, going back to Caesar's legions. At any rate, *Cinqantenaire* was an imposing backdrop to our efforts to bring a bit of cheer into soldiers' lives. The park itself was just one broad expanse of green, a suitable setting for the memorial gem. The only disturbing element was our tent city and the U. S. Army's roaring trucks, generally waiting in long lines for clearances.

Occasionally a few of our Americans were missing when it came time to return. This was not a major problem. We simply turned their names and data over to the British M. P.'s. They generally got our badly-soiled missing men a few days later. Punishment, unless a violent crime had been committed in Brussels, was turned over to the American unit where the culprit belonged.

The Brits, I thought, were much better at handling this than the American M. P.'s in Paris. In France, G.I.'s could easily disappear into the underground and join criminal gangs with black market connections. Brussels in those days had no large-scale underground or black market. Besides, it was much harder to hide as an AWOL American in British territory.

During the occupation the French embraced the black market enthusiastically. After all, they reasoned, it was the only way to keep on living and it had to hurt *les Boches*. In fact, business went well in France during the occupation; factories were busy supplying German war equipment and farmers were busy selling their produce at highly inflated prices. Even the French underground was busy--mostly fighting each other and at times, even the Germans.

My experience with the *Maquis*, one branch of the French underground, was limited to a few contacts at Brest. They were great in locating Kraut strong points. A few even joined us in the assaults. They were of less assistance in information delivery or describing what we needed to attack and at what time. In sum, I always suspected the French underground; too many played footsie with the Nazis in the past. Most of the Battalion officers thought as I did.

I suppose I joined the basic skeptics ranks at this point in my life. All of us heard of so many stories we had no way of proving or disproving, we had to take them for exactly that--stories. I know I trusted few, if any, civilians. As time progressed, however, I became more tolerant of what most of these people had been through and why some had to become habitual liars to survive. Once that barrier had been crossed I began to view their lives differently.

My first happenings after I arrived in Brussels were wild, something people can have dreams, or nightmares, of. The American officers at the Hotel Berger always stuck together even though we weren't all part of the Belgian Leave Section.

Often we would go to the area night clubs in the neighboring *Porte Louise* section of the city. We would pick up what girls were available--our choices were actually quite good when word got out that the rich Americans were buying. But we were raucous and loud and, at times, unruly. Particularly if one of our group thought he was being cheated on drink or playmate costs.

One of our favorite spots was the *Boeuf Sur le Toit*, or Cow on the Roof. A fairly spiffy, upper story joint, it had a glass block floor for a dancing area. Our first choice sport was to find a way to get below this floor for the obvious visual pleasures awaiting us. I don't think we ever did, and even if we did the glass blocks were mostly opaque. But this was our game and it became a standing challenge causing loud, uncouth toasts to visiting ladies which the management did not enjoy; the girls probably thought otherwise.

On other drinking occasions we behaved like the Wild West creatures I'm sure most Belgians thought we really were. I recall one incident where a paratroop officer and I upset a half dozen tables in a bar because we believed--and probably rightly--we had been overcharged for our drinks. We paid for the damage the next day when the Brit M. P.'s came to get us. Our only win was that we never did pay for the overpriced drinks.

About a month after I arrived several collaborator-owned apartments became available to American officers.

A certain Captain Smith (we all called him just Smitty) and I figured we could get one, particularly if he could pull one of his "you-owe-me-something-don't-you?" acts with Belgian civilian authorities.

Smitty should have been a supply sergeant. He was Air Corps, and I don't think he ever heard a shot fired in anger, but he was one of the world's great procurers. Early in our friendship he managed to get a jeep. I never asked him from where and whom, but it was there for us and our business and dates. For most of our military tasks we had civilian cars and drivers assigned and I, for one, never much trusted chauffeurs.

Our one problem with the jeep--other than the dim possibility that someone would come to claim ownership--was the British. They had a strict regulation that no civilians could ride in military vehicles, anytime, anywhere, after dark.

We frequently violated this rule and we never got caught although it was close a couple of times. I do remember one night where we were being followed by a Limey patrol. Our two dates, with their bicycles piled on the hood of the jeep--one of the girls was sitting on the bikes--managed to unload themselves and the bikes just after we rounded a corner. They were pedaling down the street and Smitty and I were sitting alone in our jeep as the patrol came up to us. We did hear a Brit lecture on the proper use of government vehicles then, but nothing else happened.

Smitty was a big man, well over six feet tall and somewhat paunchy. He was at least 15 years older than I and thousands of years older in street smarts. He was assigned to the Belgian Leave Section as Army Air Force liaison and sat with us at the intake center, supposedly taking care of his Air Force personnel. But there were so few of them coming through in comparison to the grunt soldiers that his work load was laughable. That didn't bother Smitty. He just used his idle time to become better acquainted in the Brussels area. Whenever we needed anything from the Limeys or the Belgians we just asked

Smitty to arrange it. He always knew the right button to push to handle the job.

    Smitty and I eventually were awarded a collaborator's apartment, a seven-room, three-bedroom and three-bathroom spread that was truly mind-boggling to this simple soldier. I never expected anything more than utility housing, but here was this magnificent, deluxe apartment in one of the better sections of the city, now ours. At least until the collaborator who owned it got out of jail.

    The front part contained a large living room with a 50-foot curved glass window overlooking tree-lined Boulevard San Michel. Adjoining was a large dining area with a wooden floor. We promptly denuded this room of all tables and chairs and called it our dance hall. There was also a study and a Pullman-type kitchen leading to a cozy rear balcony. Two bedrooms and a small, maid's quarters room completed the ensemble, completely furnished, kitchen semi-stocked and radio playing. It was much better than we deserved.

    We also had acquired, through Smitty of course, a homeless Dutch kid. He was anywhere from 13 to 18 years old, always smiling. He had no place to stay, he explained in his fractured English. He was what was known then as a displaced person. No one had any records on him, nor did anyone care what happened to him and the thousands of other D. P. 's, all ages, wandering through post-war Europe. He said he had no family, no home, no papers. He repeatedly said he wanted to go back to Holland, but he made no moves in that direction as long as I knew him.

    He volunteered to become our houseboy for no pay but board and room. We agreed, gave him the maid's room and he became part of our family. His name, he said, was Pietre (pronounced Pee-et-truh). He understood much more English than he let on and, at heart, he was a petty thief. But he was cheerful, ready to try anything. He actually became a fair cook and house cleaner. He loved to mix drinks at parties, always sneaking a little on the side.

    Pietre's native language was Dutch (or German) and he naturally got along well in Flemish, Belgium's other language, used extensively in bi-lingual Brussels and exclusively in the country's northern provinces.

Our apartment was on the top floor of a six-floor building, each apartment taking up an entire floor. Our "next door" neighbors, on the floor below, were a Brussels copper fabrication plant owner, Albert Geisler, and his wife, Francine. We lost no time in knocking on their door.

They were charming people and took to us immediately, as we did to them. They spoke English decently, particularly Francine, and that was a big help in getting organized in our new quarters.

My French was improving daily. I constantly read Belgian newspapers and used the language as much as I could regardless of my many mistakes. Both Albert and Francine were patient and gentle teachers.

Several evenings after meeting the Geislers we talked about the previous occupant-owner of our apartment. The Geislers didn't like him, but they did not turn him in to the Belgian Resistance who actually appropriated his apartment and put him in jail for dealing with the Germans. He owned a lumber supply firm, I believe.   Albert had a philosophic view of the situation--he said a patriot is one who is forced to do business with the enemy and makes no money at it; a collaborator is one who enjoys doing that business and worse, makes money doing it.

I wasn't really interested at that time in economics; I had my own theories telling me that most Belgians during the occupation were collaborators anyway.

One evening I asked Albert and Francine if they knew any *belles filles avec l'honneur*--"nice girls". Then I described as best I could all the attributes of the American girl-next-door as an example. I remarked that I'd had my fill of women who wanted nylon hose, cigarettes or other valuables in exchange for their company and smiles. Then they were with another guy the next night, and possibly, if they could avoid it, not for sex. Most of *les femmes* I knew tried to encourage this partying togetherness and American support-giving on a continuing basis, whatever it took on their part

Francine replied that she knew of two *infirmieres* (nurses) who loved a party but who had a difficult time getting free for an evening. They had to be back at the hospital early, she added.

That situation suited me fine and nurses sounded wonderful. Smitty was ready for anything. He wanted to call them right then. Francine said she would set up a rendezvous in our apartment which the Geislers would attend with the nurses. They would probably prefer chaperones, she stressed. Fine, we said, and the deal was set up for the coming weekend, if possible. Francine would make the arrangements.

This was a big event for us. We went all out for food, figuring that if we weren't the attraction, scarce American food probably would be. Smitty and Pietre gathered all the big band records they could find and I saw to the wine and liquor--and food. Francine had called and reported that the nurses could stay only an hour or two but they were happy to come and meet us and dance. Francine, knowing us and in particular, Smitty, emphasized the word dance for our agenda that evening.

Promptly at eight o'clock that Saturday (nurses are always on time, I learned pointedly later) in came Jacqueline Munday and her companion, a tiny one called Marie (Wawa) Watrin. Jacqueline, we learned, was a head nurse in the operating room at Edith Cavell Hospital, one of Brussel's largest private hospitals, and Nurse Wawa's aunt was *La Directrice* of Cavell.

Neither of our guests spoke much English. They were trim, attractively groomed and pleasant.. I took an instant liking to Wawa who had the better features of the two and who seemed like a little girl lost.

Jacqueline was obviously the leader. She said that both of them must be back by 10 o'clock and that didn't mean *tard par cinq ou dix minutes*. Despite this ominous beginning, we had an excellent time dancing, eating, laughing, mostly at my fractured French, and just talking.

Jackie--in time I called her that and she called me "Beel"--also seemed to be the lively one. She had clog-type shoes and she beat them on our wooden floor with rat-a-tat precision. She was a good dancer. I loved to dance somewhat wildly and we soon made a "floor show" pair.

I remember taking her into our ample kitchen later and showing her our eggs (why, I'll never know unless it was an excuse to get her away from the crowd. She probably thought I was crazy. Eggs were prized in Belgium then but they certainly were not a curiosity item). Anyway, I then managed to get her out on our back balcony and I kissed her, I'm sure somewhat passionately.

We evidently both liked it because after that monk-like evening I began seeing Jackie increasingly over the next few weeks and months. And despite the language difficulties, we did have good fun times together.

Jackie had been raised on the Belgian seashore near Ostend. Her mother, an *Ambulancier* during World War I, died of tuberculosis shortly after Jackie's birth. Jackie's father then thought it best to send his daughter to an open air health resort-school. Jackie spent 16 or 17 years there, coming back to Brussels only once or twice a year, and then, finally, to enter nursing school during the German occupation.

Jackie's father, Maurice Munday, was a Frenchman holding dual citizenship in France and Belgium. He served as a sergeant in the Belgian Army during World War I, was captured and held as a prisoner for a few months before his return to Brussels and marriage to Louise Lefevre, Jackie's mother.

He owned an automobile dealership and repair garage in Brussels between the wars. After Louise died he married again, this time to a lady named Madam Landauer who had a daughter only a year or two older than Jackie. According to Jackie, Madame didn't ever make her feel welcome in her father's newly-established household, which is the compelling reason Jackie wanted to stay at the seashore for all of those years.

When the Germans invaded Belgium in 1940, the Munday family, including Jackie, took off for southern France, where Maurice had relatives. There they stayed for several months, until the Germans told them to return to Brussels or risk losing all of their property there.

They came back to renew their lives--Jackie at nursing school, Papa (as Jackie always called him) at the garage.

Madame Landauer had her own memories of World War I--a daughter by the name of Nicole. Nicole's father, it was said softly within the family, was an American G. I. from Detroit who had never seen his daughter, never even knew he had left one in France in 1918.

There was obvious jealousy and rivalry between Nicole and Jackie--another of the reasons Jackie chose to stay away. And the southern France sojourn didn't help. When the family returned to Brussels, Nicole stayed in France with a French soldier she had met on the way, one of the 2,000,000 who dropped their weapons and fled before the Germans. Actually, many just changed clothes and became civilians.

Nicole later met and married a Swiss hotel heir and became a world traveler and eventually, after the parents had died, a friend of Jackie's and mine. She now lives in Rome with her adult son from the Swiss marriage.

My experiences with Jackie and the nurses of Edith Cavell brought me into contact with many Brits and, of course, Belgians whom I never would have met otherwise. Among these interesting people were members of a Royal Air Force fighter squadron stationed near Brussels and flying close support for British and Canadian ground troops in Holland and northern Germany. Jackie and Wawa had known them before me under much the same circumstances as they knew me--only the hospital had arranged the evenings, not Francine and Albert.

I particularly admired these pilots, not only for their considerable achievements but for their elegant nonchalance about death. It was a game with them.

Every weekend, when we saw the RAF group, a few more were missing. A simple toast was offered to the dead and absent, and that was that. Another day was coming. Just like the movies. Their attitude particularly appealed to my own fatalistic view of armed combat-- you're lucky, or you're not.

But it must have been easier for airmen. They got it fast if they were unlucky. Ground warfare produced ugliness and slow death in grime. Anything but fostering a devil-may-care attitude.

Jackie's father (at right, in uniform) was a French citizen who became, by choice, a Belgian (he lived in Brussels and had a citizenship declaration option) in the early years of World War I. He became a sergeant in the Belgian Army which so successfully resisted the Germans 30 years before my arrival. At the end of the war he married Louise Lefevre, a young ambulance worker from Brussels who was also active on that war's battlefields. Louise died of tuberculosis shortly after Jackie's birth in 1921.

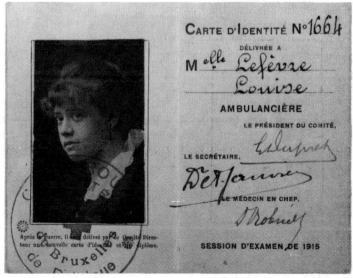

I was always curious about what Jackie did during the occupation--she worked, observed the nightly curfew and tried to avoid all of the *sal Boches* even though some of her nursing colleagues were caught after the curfew and spent the night at the German police station, she recounted. And then, after we came to know each other well, she voluntarily told me her story of the Liberation of Brussels. I thought it was a beautiful expression of what these people went through for four years--and felt when the magic moment of freedom finally came.

On the night of September 5, 1944--the same night I was wounded in Brest--the first British tanks arrived in Brussels. They were met in much the same way we were welcomed to Brittany. One big party--nothing held back.

Jackie was dancing with the Brit tankers near *Porte Namur*, an entryway to the city. Champagne, lots of singing, no understanding or language barriers even though no one understood the tankers. And yes, food--something the Belgians hadn't seen in such quantities for years. Giveaway bars of soap, too.

A British tank driver grabbed Jackie and forced her to the ground underneath his stopped tank. In effect, he raped her, quickly and thoroughly, as in an animal act.

Jackie never said a word then or later. She initially struggled and finally gave of herself in a momentary explosion of gratitude. She never saw the tank driver again, never told the story to anyone but me. I, too, understood such a release after five years of slavery-torture and told her so. She didn't grieve the memory.

There were frequent parties at Belgian homes where I met caring people. I quickly forgot my feelings of distaste, even scorn, for Belgian actions during the occupation. These patriotic Belgian citizens I got to know and like genuinely hated Germans, the people who had invaded and destroyed their country and their way of living twice within their lifetimes. After the liberation, the Belgians even threw out their king who, they felt, was too friendly with the Nazis, particularly through his commoner wife's war-profiteering family. And yes, some of them did accommodate the hated *Boche* in order to stay alive. Who wouldn't?

By this time Jackie and I were a team. She lived with two other Edith Cavell nurses, both of whom married Americans later. I was a frequent guest in their apartment and they were frequent beneficiaries of American food, including scarce fresh fruit.

The war in Europe had ended. By August, Japan was gone. I didn't care if I went home or not, I was having such a good time in Brussels. I toured Switzerland twice with my good friends, the Geislers. I spent several days in the vineyards of France. And I was busy winding down the affairs of the Belgian Leave Section.

One lovely summer day (it was seldom hot in Brussels) Jackie and I would picnic at the *Bois de Cambre*. The next we would go to the horse races and then do a weekend bicycling out to the monument to the Duke of Wellington (Napoleon was there, too) at Waterloo.

We regularly visited the elegant restaurants near the *Place de Ville* and *Manniken Pis.* We didn't miss too many bars or dance places either, and this included the infamous *Boeuf sur le Toit.* To prove Belgian hospitality, the management of that *boite de nuit* welcomed me back.

It was the good life--something Jackie and I never forgot. We tasted all the wines, sampled all the cheeses and pastry delicacies and mingled with all the beautiful people coming through Brussels. These included President Truman (on his way to the Potsdam meeting) Mr. and Mrs. Walter Cronkite, Bob Considine, Bob Hope, assorted defrocked European nobility and dozens of others who were not so noted but fun.

By this time I was running an officers club in *Hotel Centrale* in downtown Brussels and in charge of closing the famous *Onze Novembre*, the G.I. hotel near the *Gare du Nord*. *Onze Novembre* became the principal jumping off place to explore Brussels for our wartime G.I.'s.

My duties at the officers club included hiring jazz bands, mostly from Holland, and contracting for entertainment from all over Europe. It even embraced cognac buying trips to France. Never, except by the strangest roll of the dice, could a boy soldier from Iowa expect something like this Shangri-La in his lifetime.

Reality always strikes back, and in early 1946 I

received orders to return to the states. By this time I was truly torn about whether or not to take my discharge in Europe and stay. In the end, a longing to see home again won the day.

I remember when I told Jackie. It was a cold day in February. We went into the unheated front room of her apartment on *Rue Vanderkinderer* to look at some street commotion below. It was nothing, but I seized the opportunity to write *Jackie et Beel* (I always teased her about her pronunciation of Bill) on the frosted window.

Then I told her about the orders, that I would be leaving for home shortly. I remember saying that I didn't know what America was like now but that I was going to explore life there for a time. There was a good chance I would come back to Europe, I said.

If I found a job which would support both of us, I added, I would send for her. Would she wait? And would she consider coming to America?

She didn't hesitate over this half-assed marriage proposal. She said she would wait to hear from me--and that remained our pledge until we were joined in marriage in New York a little over a year later.

THEN . . . .

. . . . and now

Francine and Albert Geisler of Brussels (above left, shown relaxing in someone's backyard with the author) became good friends--as did many Belgians who knew Jackie, who appears at right above *avec son lieutenant*. Below is the night copy desk of *The Omaha World-Herald,* shortly after I joined it in 1946. I'm the one with the phone.

Jackie was a huge import treasure for the Arendt family. She was smart, disciplined and hard-working. And she demanded those same virtues from the rest of us. Convent educated and reared, Jackie never had much of a home life, but she raised the boys mostly by herself, only resuming her nursing career when they were in their late teens. If anthing, the house was organized--laundry had to be in by Wednesday, rooms clean by the weekend. And rather than suffer male inefficiency, she preferred to do most or all the chores herself. She always had trouble with the English language, and never lost her French accent. She was embarrassed by this--others thought it charming. She learned to drive in America, but she never could get used to left turns in traffic. So she charted in her mind how to get places using right turns only. Son Bill remembers some odd routes, but, he said, she never missed the mark. Jackie liked to socialize, but her primary interest was home and family. At center, Jackie is reading to Bill and below, at a family patio picnic in August, 1965.

Epilogue

_Restarting. . . Probably the most important thing
we did in WWII was to come home and
quietly rebuild our lives. . ._

*I*t took the Army a considerable time to get rid of
me. Upon arrival at Camp Kilmer, N. J., in the early spring
of 1946--via slow Liberty boat (maybe one of the cargo
ships I helped build in California, almost a lifetime ago)--I
was ordered to Camp McCoy in Wisconsin for discharge.
There I was informed that because I was still carried as
"limited service," I had to appear before another board for
reclassification or retirement.

The Army could not discharge any of its non-
regular service people as handicapped in any way, they
explained. It was either general service or, as mostly in the
case of regular Army personnel injured in the line of duty,
full retirement with all the pension and care benefits
attendant. Not much chance for the latter option, I
reasoned.

So McCoy shipped me to the Army hospital at
Hyde Park in South Chicago, later to become a Veterans
Administration hospital. I remembered the building as an
up-scale hotel near the University of Chicago. It was not
one of my stops in earlier years, although we did hit South
Chicago regularly to visit pre-war black-and-tan watering
holes. None of these older negro-white spots remained, I
discovered during my post-war stay at Hyde Park.

Languishing in my old home town while awaiting

board review was not the worst of duties. I hastened to renew friendships at Northwestern University on the other side of town--but never, I thought, too far away for old buddies.

Except there weren't any around. It was as if an entire generation had disappeared. Instead, fuzz-cheeked cherubs occupied the classrooms. I dated a couple of the female variety but found the small talk boring. They were considerably more than a generation apart from my war-baptized classmates. I was only four or five years older than these people, I reasoned, but I didn't understand them and I'm just as positive they didn't understand me.

Certainly veterans came back to complete their education later. Even more took advantage of the G. I. Bill and started college. But they weren't around in any significant numbers in the spring of 1946. I've often wondered how the ex-G.I.'s handled their relations with non-veterans (or vice versa) after World War II. But that's probably another story, dealing with the same problems every returning, war-burned generation faced.

In due course I had my board hearing (by this time I just wanted out; before I had thought that if the Army wanted to keep me maybe I should stay in, if I could return to Europe). The doctors examined my hand, questioned me on future plans and careers and, within minutes, ruled that I was not eligible for retirement. I would be discharged as fit for general service; anything the Army owed me for my wounds would be available through the newly-established Veterans Administration, they said.

Then it was back to McCoy for my discharge and a few days later, a final trip on Uncle Sam to LeMars, Iowa, from whence I entered the service three-and-a-half years earlier.

I arrived in LeMars via the Illinois Central Railroad in the middle of a bright spring morning. No one was around to greet me, but that was my doing. I hadn't let anyone know my arrival time.

Still, it was strange to walk down the tracks in the middle of town, in uniform, my barracks bag on my shoulder, and not see any one I knew or who knew me. Or even anyone who said "hello".

A bum or two lolling beside the tracks just looked at me. I looked back, just as challenging. Even the sights of LeMars were strange until I got to where the tracks crossed Central Avenue and the Royal Theater and next door, the Billy Arendt Hat Shop, were in view. The welcome was tumultuous when I walked into my parents' store. The only child, prodigal son and hope for carrying on the family name had returned!

For lack of something better to do that summer, I took a course in accounting at Western Union College (the name change to Westmar came a bit later).

Most of my time was spent at the local airport where I took flying lessons and earned my pilot's license. I guess I remembered those beautiful bomb release peel-offs of our P-47's and the attitudes on life expressed by my RAF friends as something I admired and wanted to emulate, even in a small way.

All this time I was writing to Jackie in Brussels, saying with increasing frequency that as soon as I got a respectable job I would send for her. I was anything but a laid-back recluse in LeMars, but I never found anyone to compare with Jackie.

In late August and September I took a trip to Kansas (my mother's old grounds) to look for a newspaper job. My reception in Topeka was tepid but Kansas City was encouraging. I told them I would send some writing samples and headed for home via Omaha. On a chance and knowing no one there, I called on *The World-Herald*-- and basically was hired on the spot. My Medill School background sold me to Fred Ware, Managing Editor. I told him not to expect much at the start; I was four years from any newspaper experience. But it was a start--mostly offered because of a hiring hunch of Fred's--so that I became what I had been educated for: A newsman. I started on the job the next Monday. Just time enough to get to LeMars and back with my clothes.

If the prospecting trip had not paid off in interest, or a job, I had already promised myself that I would go back to school under the G. I. Bill and get my law degree.

And that undoubtedly would have delayed plans with Jackie.

I began working the night copy desk and the central police station. In fact, I was for a couple of years the only man the nightside had on the streets. That meant coverage of all dignitaries arriving after 4 P. M., plus the mashed potato and pea dinner meeting-speaking circuit. And despite the rust and general lack of know-how I knew within two months that I could make it as a journalist. I asked Jackie to come over in one of our prolonged overseas telephone calls.

She agreed--and then the paperwork started. It took us a good three months to process what was a simple immigration, not a war bride procedure. The Belgians had never filled their immigration quotas to the United States, but that didn't seem to stop our bureaucrats from having their prolonged say. At least it seemed that way to me. But everything finally came together--on short notice.

Jackie was scheduled to dock in New York on a Saturday. I took off from Omaha in my father's borrowed 1941 Ford on a Wednesday after work, actually a Thursday at 2 A. M. Luckily, I had agreed to take an acquaintance into the big city with me. He did most of the driving that first 18 hours, when we made Pennsylvania. Believe it or not, we were in New York at dockside when Jackie's Holland-America Lines Veendam came in late that morning.

We were married May 8, 1947 at St. Patrick's Cathedral in New York (or rather, in the rectory at the rear of the Cathedral). Jackie's fellow boat passengers came to the small affair, as did a couple of my friends in the city. Marie (Wawa) Watrin, married to Kenny Heil of Allentown, Pennsylvania, another ex-G. I., was our Matron of Honor. Our honeymoon was the drive back to Omaha, via stops to see friends at Lake Wawasee in Indiana and in LeMars to see my folks.

I remember our arrival in Omaha, in early June, 1947. It was snowing! I can imagine what Jackie was thinking about then. She had had a cram course tour on America over the past month and I'm sure not all of it was easy. Particularly meeting my folks and spending some time in LeMars with relatives and friends--all that and not understanding the language. After seeing the big snowflakes coming down in her new home in June, no less, she could at least recall kinder and gentler times in Europe.

Jackie spent her last evening in Brussels as a dinner guest of the Belgian Prince Regent Charles. He remembered he had hidden at Edith Cavell Hospital during the Belgian surrender in the early 1940's and that Jackie was one of his caretakers. He also knew she was leaving for America to marry an ex-G. I.

Jackie recounted that an aide to the Regent had called her apartment and issued the invitation in, of course, very formal tones. She was flabbergasted--it was for the following evening, at the Royal castle.

At the appointed hour a limousine picked her up at her apartment and took her to the palace for the personal dinner with Prince Charles. She said he knew all about me, where I was from, what I did for a living, how long I had known her, everything. He evidently had his people do some investigating. Apparently I passed the Royal inspection.

Prince Charles wished Jackie well. Jackie told me later that he invited several other Edith Cavell nurses he knew to dinner if they were leaving the country or getting married. Never, at any time during the evening, was he alone with her, Jackie said, and her friends reported the same precautions. Anyway, I thought this was a beautiful farewell gesture on the part of the Prince Regent.

My new wife jump-started her second career in nursing shortly after our arrival in Omaha. She began as a student nurse in Bishop Clarkson Hospital, working the night shift. When she received her nursing certificate along with her citizenship papers a year or so later, she became a primary care nurse and completed her career at Nebraska Methodist Hospital. She never went back to her operating room specialty ("I prefer to take care of people") and she never returned to Europe ("There's nothing for me there now").

My career as a newspaperman ended in 1953 when I left *The World-Herald's* business news desk to enter the world of public relations. Five years later, I started my own PR consulting and advertising agency firm.

Jackie and I also raised a family in Mid-America. Bill, our first son, was born in 1951 and is now a telemarketing sales and operations executive. Our second son, Steve, was born in 1956. He is now Director of Pharmacy at the E. A. Conway Medical Center, actually a teaching hospital and part of the Louisiana State University system, in Monroe, Louisiana. Both of them have earned master's degrees during their working careers. They also helped to produce four grandchildren, three boys and a girl.

Jackie died in 1988 following a prolonged kidney illness. She was active in patient care nursing until her last years.

My hand and knee never gave me major troubles. That, again, was luck--but part of it may have come from some good advice I received from a medical man while I was still in the service: "You'll get along better if you don't pay any attention to your hand, and don't let other people pay attention to it either."

Just one final note before I close this account of a citizen-soldier, written some 50-plus years after the event: This story is probably typical of my generation and not so different from the thousands of stories which could be extracted from any veterans' group of my vintage.

We are not heroes despite some attempts to make us gallant. We did what we had to do and what anyone in our situation would do, and, as Colonel Cawthon said, we didn't give it a great deal of thought at the time.

Probably the most important thing we did was to come home and more or less quietly rebuild our lives, probably five years behind in our career paths but even more years ahead in living experiences.

I like to think our actions in war and particularly, in peace, may have helped America become the powerful nation it is today. And what's more, even with all the misery and pain--yes, and the joy--my generation would probably do it all over again!

Happy piloting days in LeMars (left)--I finally got to do those beautiful chandelles. Below, with father, mother and Jackie and, early on, with my two boys.

Somewhat later, with the same two guys. I was known as the Oft-Absent Ogre during their schoolboy years, but thanks to their mother, the strict disciplinarian Belgian and her "wait until I tell your father" French-accented approach to family discipline, they survived. The two boys are quite different in temperament--Bill (on the left) is a son of the 1960's, something of a free spirit, and Steve, five years younger, is Mr. Straight Arrow. He stands taller, too.

This is the entire family, circa 1998. Standing (left to right) are Abbey Hoesing (Nancy Arendt's daughter); Colin Arendt, Son Steven's oldest; Nancy, William Munday Arendt, oldest son and husband of Nancy; W. Kyle Arendt, Bill's oldest, and Steven. Seated are (left to right) Alison Arendt, Bill's youngest; Bill Sr., and his friend, Shirley Shick; Wesley Hoesing and T. J. Arendt, Steven's youngest.

Index

If you would like to order additional copies of this book, please contact:

PRA, inc.
12631 Manderson Plaza
Omaha, Nebraska 68164
(402) 493-0771
Fax (402) 493-0771*44

$11.90 ea., plus $3 handling and shipping

Also by William F. Arendt:

The Man from Worms--*an inspiring personal story of business and family success in America's heartland from Fred Bosselman, the Grandaddy of the Truck Stoppers. Plus a discussion of 7 quality factors to look for in your dealings with others.*

Lucky--*a story of Chuck Durham, his family and HDR, a world leader in architectural-engineering services.*

(This is as a particpating author, writing on the growth years of HDR)